Your

Horoscope

in

Your

Hands

Lorna Green

The Wessex Astrologer

Published in 2008 by
The Wessex Astrologer Ltd
4A Woodside Road
Bournemouth
BH5 2AZ
England

www.wessexastrologer.com

Copyright © Lorna Green

ISBN 9781902405377

A catalogue record of this book is available at The British Library

Cover design by Dave at Creative Byte, Poole, Dorset

Printed and bound in the UK by MPG Biddles Ltd, Kings Lynn, Norfolk.

ACKNOWLEDGEMENTS

I would like to thank Roy MacKinnon and Liz Seddon of the Bristol School of Astrology, where I obtained my Diploma in Astrology. They are talented astrologers, and very generous with their knowledge. I would also like to thank the anonymous people who have allowed me to use their data.

CONTENTS

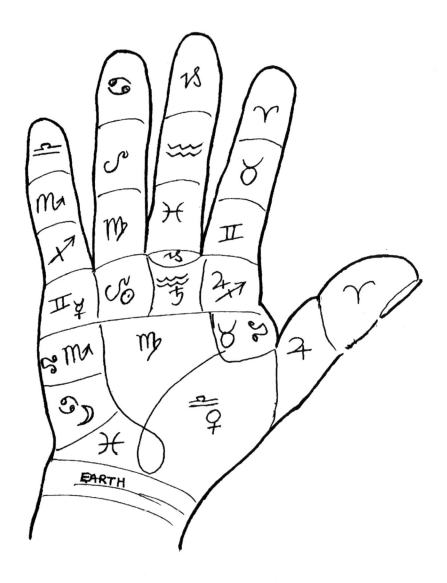

This figure shows the areas of the hand traditionally governed by
the signs and planets

INTRODUCTION

Every astrological chart is unique. The planets progress in their repeating orbits around the Sun, but the exact combinations of the angles they form to one another is unrepeatable. Each chart has its own individual planetary geometry, its own character and identity.

Hands also are formed of a unique combination of characteristics. It has long been observed that there is a correspondence between astrology and chiromancy. Just as astrologers divide a chart into sections, or houses, so the hand is divided into areas, each of which is seen to correspond to the planets and their signs. How a planet sits in a chart, how beneficially or inharmoniously it is aspected, is reflected in the shape, the relatively prominent areas, the lines and skin ridges of each hand.

The frontispiece picture is of a traditional view of the hand and how it reflects planetary influence. We nowadays consider the central band across the palm to be the domain of Mars, (see further on page 32). As an extension to Chinese acupuncture, there is a machine available which is used to treat patients through specific areas of the hand. The machine emits a small electrical current, which is directed to whichever area of the hand reflects the astrological area requiring healing.

Both the astrological chart, and the hand, must be interpreted in relation to the backdrop of social conditions, nationality, and the current zeitgeist, the prevailing collective beliefs and feelings. The outer planets, with their long orbits, can have a generational influence; they give an indication of currently prevailing conditions. French astrologer André Barbault, born in 1921, concluded that when the outer planets are closest to each other, from our geocentric viewpoint on Earth, or the heliocentric viewpoint from our Sun, then generally chaotic conditions on Earth are more likely.

Genetic conditions of heredity also show themselves in the hand; for instance some southern European nationals commonly display a very flexible thumb, with the top section bending back almost at right angles. The long, lissom bodies of many African nationals are reflected in their very long hands.

When looking at a chart or at a hand, the important matter to note is whether there is anything which stands out as uncharacteristic. The chart may show contradictions, layers of personality; it may show a planet which stands away from the rest and could be very difficult to express or integrate. Study of the hand can confirm how this is working out. Just as with the natal chart, uncharacteristic lines or features on the hand are areas which could present problems.

For an astrologer, it is not possible to be certain how transits have actually been experienced, although we can gauge what the most probable response might be. It is the hand which shows the effect on the person. It is unusual for the main lines of a hand to change, although they may extend or contract to some extent, or their condition may alter. The minor lines, the skin ridges, and the condition of the lines and hand all respond and leave their mark. This information is most valuable to astrologer and palmist alike, and this book aims to show the parallels between the chart and the hand.

PART 1

TAKING HANDPRINTS

IDENTIFYING THE LINES AND CHARACTERISTICS OF THE HAND

RELATIONSHIPS

MONEY

HEALTH

Left Hand or Right Hand?

There is often confusion about which hand should be referred to when reading a palm. The popular saying that "The left hand is the one you are born with, and the right hand is what you make of it" has some basis in fact.

Some people have a firm belief that in the case of a right-handed person it would be the right hand which would show the changing lines and current influences, whilst the left hand would remain the same. This opinion holds that for a left-handed person the reverse would be the case, with the left hand showing most changes. I can only state that, in my experience, it has been the right hand which shows more changes. I do not dispute the experience of others, and I do suggest that you always study both hands. One hand will show itself to represent most closely the birth chart, while the other may well have more lines and marks, representing experiences. The hands of a 'fixed' or stubborn and intractable person would not be expected to show as many changes as those of a more fluctuating personality. In the case of the 'fixed' person, any major changes will be of much greater significance, and must be taken seriously. (See also Changing Lines page 47.)

The 'static' hand, which I have found to be the left hand, can in fact change. The markings represent more ingrained characteristics, as would be shown by the natal chart, and any changes to its lines and conditions represent rather deep changes and developments to that person, whereas the 'receptive' hand shows more readily the evidence of life's experience and the effects on the mental and physical condition, effects which may pass without leaving ingrained marks such as would be laid down on the 'static' hand. This explains the saying above, that the left hand is the one you are born with – as the natal chart – and the right hand is what you make of it, how you experience transits and progressions to that chart.

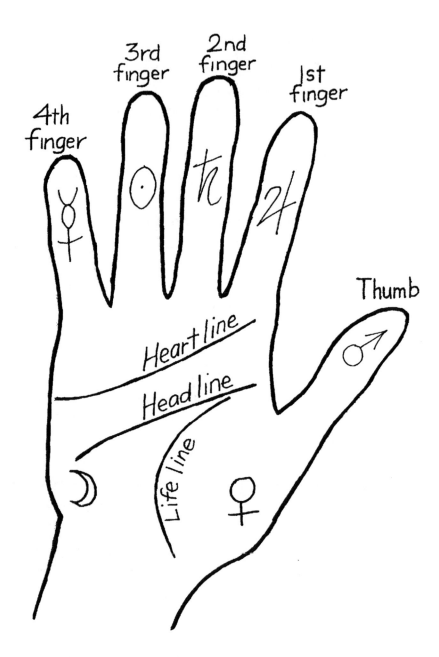

This figure shows the basic lines and the modern associations
with the planets

Taking Hand Prints

To be most useful, a handprint needs to show as much detail as possible. Not only the main lines are needed, but also the skin ridge patterns should be clearly visible, as well as the finest lines. An easy way to achieve a really clear and permanent print is to use an ink pad and roller.

Various inkpads are readily available in stationery and art and craft shops, along with hard rollers. A two-inch wide roller is quite adequate for the job. Wider rollers are available, but as the ink pads can be bought in a three-inch wide size, this seems to be the most economical option. Ink pads are made in permanent or washable ink. Long term staining of the hands is not the favourite option, so using the small craft supply ink pads means that you can usually clean the hands by washing with soap and water. It is not necessary to use a special hand cleaner.

The application of the ink, and the detail in the final print, seem most successful if the hands are clean, but not freshly washed. There is always a temptation to wash the hands before taking a print, but in fact a clearer print comes from a hand with a normal level of grease and moisture, and that small barrier given by the light level of grease will also make cleaning the hands easier after the print has been taken. Make sure the whole palm and fingers are well covered by ink from the roller. There is no need to apply much pressure. The skin ridge patterns need to show up on the print, so the ink should not fill the spaces between these ridges.

When the hand is placed onto the sheet of white paper it should be put down in a relaxed and uncontrived way, showing how the fingers naturally stand close to or away from each other, and the natural angle of the thumb. It is often a good idea to shake the hand for a few seconds before putting it onto the paper. This way it is more likely to be relaxed. Once on the paper it must not be moved, of course, as this would smudge the print.

Sometimes parts of the hand do not show up in the print because the profile is higher in some parts than in others; for instance, if the Mounts of Venus and the Moon are high and full, and the middle of the hand is thin, then it may be difficult to get a print of that middle portion of the palm. In this case one good trick is to run the hand, on the sheet of paper, back across a rolling pin to make the centre of the hand touch the paper. Another way is to press with your own fingers, through the paper, to make sure that all the hand leaves its mark. There may be some unsatisfactory prints at first, but the technique is not difficult to master, and when you come to look at the print in detail then you will see where you need to pay more attention.

One way to get a good view of the fine details on a hand is to dust it with talcum powder. Rub it in very gently, with a light touch, or the details will become blurred as the image becomes uniform. This works in the opposite way to rolling ink onto the surface of the skin ridges. It fills the gaps and not the high spots. It will not give a print, but is a very useful and immediate way of studying a hand, and is easily cleaned off.

Whether you are working from a print or straight from looking at the hand itself, a magnifying glass will be helpful in seeing the finest details.

Does the Print Tell All?

There is a great deal of information to be gleaned from a good handprint, but it cannot tell you all you need to know. Keep a mental or physical check-list of points to note, such as:

a)   The temperature of the hand. Is it hot, or cold? This gives an indication of health and circulation, and of fiery or cool temperament.

b)   The outline of the hand, and the thickness of the fingers, may not be clear from the print. It can be a very good idea to make a pencil line around the whole of the hand and fingers for a clear reference. Be sure to keep the pencil very close to the outline.

c)   How does the texture of the skin feel? Fine lines on a hard-skinned hand are out of character and therefore have much more significance than those on very fine-skinned sensitive hands.

e)   Check how full the Mounts are, and if they are soft and flabby, firm, or hard and coarse.

f)   The centre of the hand, the Plain of Mars, may be either thin or thick in profile through the hand, and this will not show up on the print. It may make the print more difficult to take if it is thin and laying between a high and full Mount of Venus and Lunar Mount, but once you have the print then you would not know its thickness unless you had felt it and noted it. Feel through the hand, from the palm to the back of the hand, gauge its thickness, and thus what strength and energy is available there.

g)   Just as with a thin Plain of Mars, there may be parts of the fingers which do not show up on the first print, where they have not touched the paper. Figure 1 (a) is an example of this. Much of the 4th, Mercury, finger, has not touched the paper, and the 2nd and 3rd fingers have not touched the paper at their base. The suggestion here is that the fingers are stiff and inflexible, that they do not bend backwards easily. This is another useful character indication.

h)   The nails cannot be seen from a palm print. Always make a note of their character, the shape and physical condition, because they give information about temperament and health.

i)   Check the Mars area on the back of the hand by holding the thumb against the 1st, Jupiter, finger. If there is a good solid fleshy mount which rises on the back of the hand beside the thumb then this indicates a robust state of health and vigour.

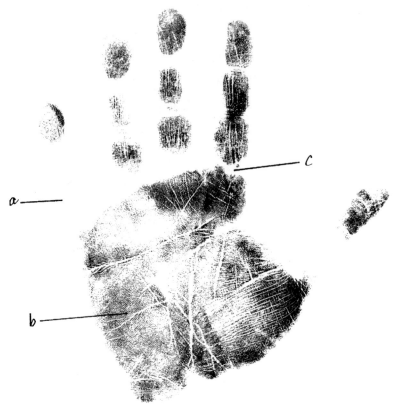

Figure 1

Figure 1 (b) shows a line across the Mount of Lunar. The line is thin and wavy, and rather confusing. Closer inspection shows that the skin ridge pattern runs straight through this line as if it were not there. In fact this line is a scratch. At the base of the Jupiter finger, figure 1 (c) is an unclear blotch, and this is actually a long-term scar. Look for marks which could be injuries, and ask for confirmation. Always consider if the lines are in character with the shape of the hand as any uncharacteristic lines or markings are especially significant. Likewise fingers or thumbs which appear not to be in tune with the dominant element. Also, the natal chart may be showing perhaps a singleton or peregrine planet, a planet may be 'out of bounds' by declination (more than 23 degrees above the ecliptic), or transits may be causing added stress.

The Elements

The twelve signs, and their ruling planets, are divided into four elements: Fire, Air, Earth and Water. Each has a self explanatory character, and the balance between them in a chart affects how the temperament can determine the way that the planets are likely to function. If there is an overload of, or a lack of one element, the whole temperamental bias can cause real problems. Some of the chart examples given demonstrate this. The elements are divided thus:

SIGN	RULING PLANET	ELEMENT
Aries	Mars	Fire
Taurus	Venus	Earth
Gemini	Mercury	Air
Cancer	Moon	Water
Leo	Sun	Fire
Virgo	Mercury	Earth
Libra	Venus	Air
Scorpio	Pluto	Water
Sagittarius	Jupiter	Fire
Capricorn	Saturn	Earth
Aquarius	Uranus	Air
Pisces	Neptune	Water

Each element has its own characteristic – the enthusiasm of Fire, the mental communication of Air, the solidity of Earth, and the emotional fluctuations of Water. Figures 2, 3, 4 and 5 illustrate the basic hand types which go with the basic elements.

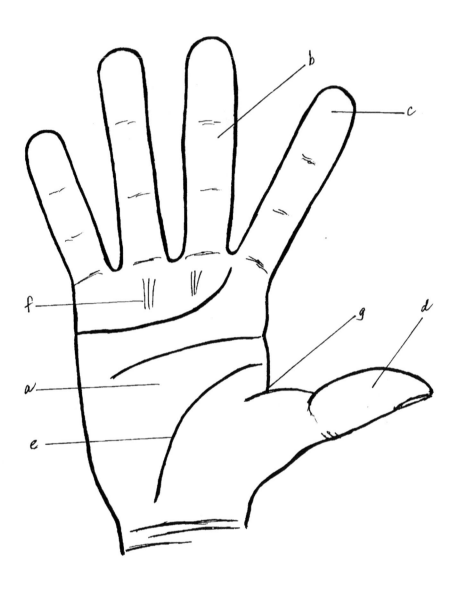

Figure 2 Fire Hand

Fire

If, for example, the Ascendant and several of the personal planets (Sun, Moon, Mercury, Venus, Mars) are in the Fire signs, then one would expect the nature and behaviour to be typically 'fiery', that is enthusiastic, initiatory, adventurous, forward looking, possibly selfish, proud and keen to follow its own desire. Expect to see a hand with a bold thumb, with fingers spreading out at the tips, reaching out for fresh experience (figure 2).

Look out for:

a)   palm narrower than fingers

b)   fingers spreading, reaching out

c)   top phalange of fingers longest

d)   thumb top phalange arrowhead shape

e)   main lines well formed and positive

f)   well-marked minor lines representing interests and activity

g)   thumb extended at wide angle to hand

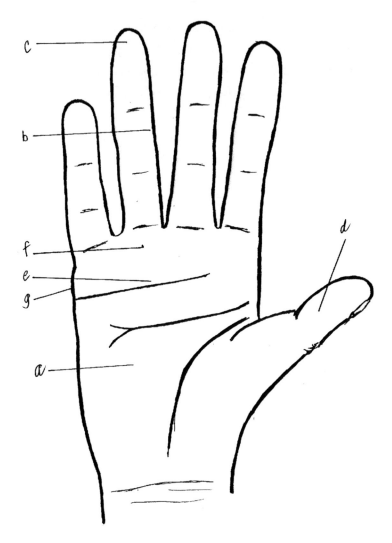

Figure 3 Air Hand

Air

A high proportion of Air in the natal chart suggests a person who lives much in his thoughts, on a mental level. Communication is important to the Gemini, relating is a fundamental urge to the Libran, and for the Aquarian expect an individualistic and innovative thought pattern. Uranus is, after all, the higher octave of Mercury. Smooth fingers indicate a thought process which can be very fast, but this speed of thought does not necessarily reflect a high level of intelligence. Information may be absorbed so quickly that it may seem intuitive. This is not the same as the dreamy intuition of a Water person. In fact, those with short smooth fingers may come to their conclusions so immediately that they can be impatient with those who ponder. Longer smooth fingers reflect more patience (figure 3).

Look out for:

a)   fine skin texture

b)   fingers fine with straight edges

c)   finger tips rounded

d)   thumb long

e)   main lines straight – air is rational, not emotional

f)   fine hyperactivity lines normal

g)   firm bump on percussion edge, under 4th (Mercury) finger suggests a 'fidget' who has difficulty in relaxing enough to stop activity

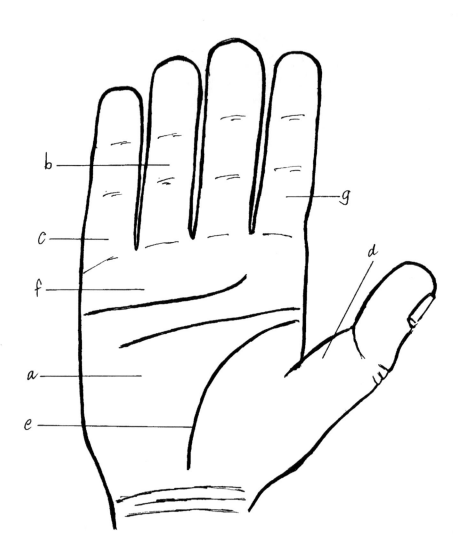

Figure 4 Earth Hand

Earth

A natal chart with a strong Earth element influence is demonstrated by a hand which is solid-looking, broad and square or rectangular. A longer, rectangular hand shows a more thoughtful person, less confined to mere basic practicalities than the short, square hand. Many very fine lines would be out of character for this type, and demonstrate a higher degree of stress than the same amount of fine lines on a Water or Air hand (figure 4).

Look out for:

a)   palm broad and firm, square or oblong

b)   fingers solid and firm

c)   bottom phalange may be longer

d)   thumb evenly balanced

e)   main lines well marked

f)   few finely-marked minor lines

g)   whole hand may lean towards thumb edge

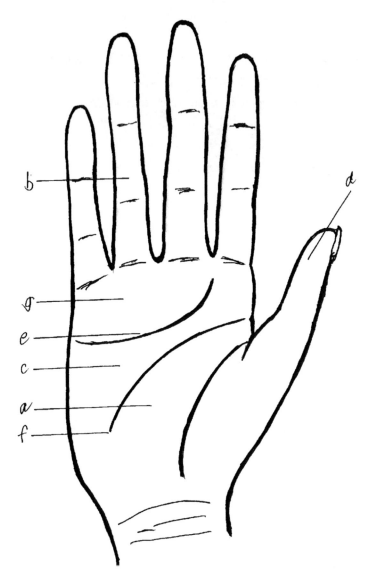

Figure 5 Water Hand

Water

This hand is typically longer and softer, in extremity appearing as if it had no bones within (no structure). On this hand it would be normal to see a preponderance of fine lines and a more pronounced Lunar area (figure 5).

Look out for:

a)   palm long and thin

b)   fingers long and weak

c)   whole hand soft, not muscular

d)   thumb long, joint not pronounced

e)   main lines curved, maybe faintly marked – Water is emotional, not rational

f)   head line curves into Mount of Lunar

g)   many fine lines normal

Figure 31 (page 81) gives an example of an extreme Water hand, showing morbid suicidal tendencies.

The dominance of any one element above the others will inevitably give the person a stronger degree of its characteristics. For instance, if there is a grand trine (120 degrees) in the chart, then it is probable that all the involved planets will be in the same element. The absence of any one element can lead to a very difficult lack of balance, and consequent psychological problems. Some case studies are given in the section on chart examples.

I had a client who had given me her birth data over the telephone. When she arrived an immediate alarm bell rang. She did not look or behave at all as I had expected. She appeared to be a very Earthy woman, had broad, solid hands, and on her Lunar Mount there was even a Loop of Nature in the skin ridge pattern (see figure 11 – Loops). She told me she loved ecology and conservation and that she spent much time gardening. The natal chart had no Earth influence in it. I tried to rectify her chart to see if we could make sense of the conflicting information. In her case, adjusting the birth time did not help. I picked out major transits from the past to see if they tied up with events in her life. The only transit she recognised was when Pluto transited natal Saturn, which surely could not have passed unnoticed, even though it would have affected many of her contemporaries. She told me it was the time when her sister had been very ill and had died. She then told me that she had never actually seen her own birth certificate; the data was what she had been told. Without some reliable birth data there was nowhere to go with the astrology. The truth may emerge when the time is right, but without the birth data that timing could not be even guessed at.

Checking the basic shape of the hand and comparing it to the elemental balance of the natal chart is a simple way to confirm the likely correctness of the birth data. Small adjustments to the birth time can change the element of the Ascendant and the angles, and of the Moon, giving quite a different balance to the elements.

Skin Texture

There is a common misconception that hard skin is always the result of rough physical work, and that fine skin belongs to those who do not use their hands. This is not essentially true, although those with tough skin are more likely to find themselves doing manual work in their life, and those with the finest skin are more likely to be less physical. This is because the texture of the skin on the palm and fingers reflects to a large extent the temperament and physical constitution. Firm skin reflects a robust, unflustered outlook, whereas a very fine skin belongs to someone with a much more sensitive system. Psychics, or people with sensitive intuition, usually have a very fine skin, on which it would be normal to see quite a quantity of fine lines.

As in all cases, the basic type of hand dictates what type of skin texture to expect. For example, on an Earth type hand it would be normal that the skin be firmer and rougher than on an Air or Water type hand. When the skin texture does not match the character of the hand then always look for contradiction in the chart. In extreme cases, a fine, shiny skin, or a rough, dry skin may be a signal that the thyroid is not functioning well and could need attention.

The Birth Time

If the character of a hand does not match the balance of elements suggested in the natal chart then the birth time given may not be correct. The suggestions given in the hand give clues which can be used to reach a more accurate birth time, and thus rectify the chart.

The circle of the Earth, and of the chart, is based on the 360-degree circle. As the Earth makes one complete rotation in a 24-hour period it follows that the eastern horizon point, the Ascendant for northern hemisphere latitudes, progresses at an approximate rate of 1 degree of arc for each 4 minutes of time. That is a movement each hour of 15 degrees, half of a complete house sign in the case of the equal house system.

As the Ascendant sign changes, so does the element. The Moon, which moves at approximately 12 to 13 degrees in each 24-hour period, may well also change sign and/or house. The change of the Moon's position in planetary geometry indicates a completely different emotional response, and if it also changes sign and element it can be a very useful tool for working out the right birth time. The rectification process can then proceed in consultation with the client, checking the timing of major transits to the Moon, the angles of the chart, and secondary progressions of the Moon.

When there is no knowledge of the birth time it is a useful practice to set up the chart for 12 noon; thereby the Moon should not be more than 6 degrees out – half of the 12 to 13 degrees of its daily passage.

The Moon's placement in a chart tells of the emotional character of the subject. It gives a pointer to early emotional conditioning of the child, of the maternal influence, habitual responses, and where one subsequently feels secure.

As an example, perhaps at the beginning of the day the Moon is placed in Leo, and it may change sign, into Virgo, during the course of the day. There is a great difference in the emotional responses of someone with the Moon in Leo to those of a person with the Moon in early Virgo. Of course, the planetary aspects made by the Moon, and the aspects the Moon makes with the angles of the chart also must be taken into account. Leo is a Fire sign, and the Moon's influence here is likely to result in a dramatic emotional response, even if the drama is 'all in the head'. There could be a level of pride (Leo – the lion), which leads a person to behave in such a way that does not offend his own personal pride. He would not find it easy to do something of which he is not proud, which would be considered beneath him.

When the Moon moves into Virgo it not only changes sign but it changes element also. Virgo is an Earth sign, ruled by Mercury which introduces a mental influence. For the first 4 degrees of a sign, the first duad, there is a greater influence of the sign's effect. Someone with the Moon in the first duad of Virgo will probably show pronounced Virgoan emotional responses. That person is likely to be a perfectionist and may be over-critical. They may well have an innate sensitivity to foodstuffs and substances, reflecting the strong effect of Virgo on the digestive system, where the body analyses intake.

In both cases, with the Moon in Leo and the Moon in Virgo, there can be a setting of high standards, but each has a different motivation. With Leo there is a personal pride. This may show up in the hand as a strong, even inflated, Jupiter finger. With the Moon in Virgo the high standard is set by an analytical, critical perfectionism. This can show in the fingernails, specifically a small 4th (Mercury) fingernail (see Fingernails, example 'f' page 25). In each case, the heart line would be expected to rise across the hand into the Mount of Jupiter and even up to the base of that finger, illustrating the aspiration to reach a high standard.

There is no degree at which a planet begins working for the next sign, as is the case with a planet approaching the next house. The distinction between one sign and another is absolute.

Example of Rectification by Moon's Position

The handprint and chart given for this example (figures 6 and 7) had only an approximate birth-time.

At 01:17 GMT the Moon moved from Aries into Taurus. The Sun is in Leo. If both the Sun and the Moon had been in Fire signs (Leo and Aries), there would have been a strong Fire influence. Study of the hand shows that the flesh is firm and solid and the hand is practical-looking. The fingers are not splayed out in an expansive way (a), and the thumb is not set at a very wide, adventurous angle (b). The bottom phalanges of the fingers are pronounced (c), suggesting a sensual nature

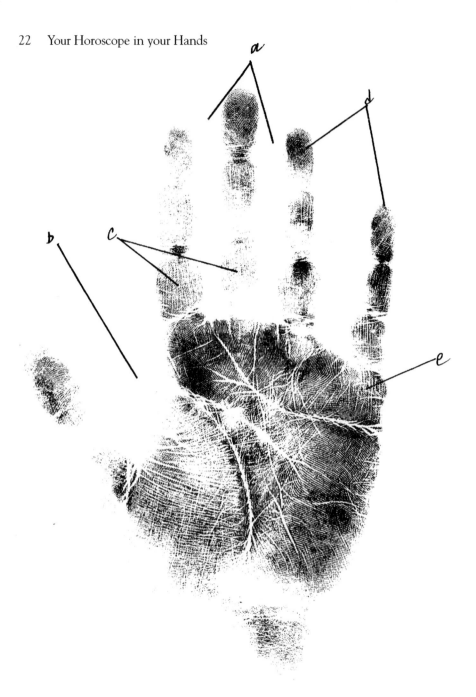

Figure 6

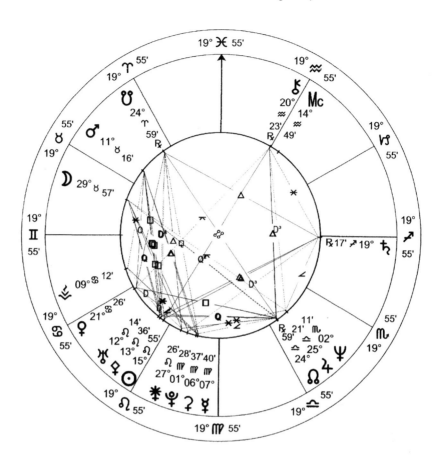

Figure 7 Chart rectification by Moon

which would enjoy physical comforts (Taurus). The fingertip patterns, mostly looped arches (d), suggest a nature which would be open to others' points of view, in accord with the Gemini Ascendant, which in itself suggests a communicative person. Also on the hand are strong sensitivity 'Samaritan' lines (e), on the Mount of Mercury, under the Mercury finger. The person's profession is caring for and nursing those less fortunate. If there had been a very strong Fire influence from both luminaries then there could have been a more adventurous, selfish and less patient attitude. Chiron in opposition to the Sun also gives the sign of the healer, but this would not have been changed by small alterations in the birth time.

At 3 minutes past mid-day the Moon would have been on the Ascendant and just into the 1st house. The client did not have health problems in infancy (a possibility with the Moon in that position), and as she works in a hospital, and hospitals are a 12th house concern, it seems that Moon in 12th house is appropriate. She feels comfortable in the hospital environment.

Until 00:39 on the birth day Mars would have been in the 12th house, the cusp of which would then have been 11 degrees of Taurus. Even up until 00:50, when the cusp of the 12th house would have been 14° Taurus 30, Mars could have been considered as working for the 12th house. She wants to help the community with her energy, not work alone.

All this information has narrowed the birth time to a point between 00:50 (Mars in 12th house before this time) and 01:17 (Moon in Aries after this time). With Sun just a degree from the IC, reinforcing her love of home and family security told by Moon in Taurus, the timing seems most likely. Saturn, on the Descendant, is working for the 7th house. Sagittarius is on the cusp of the 7th house. Her partners have been foreign and there has been an age difference.

CHARACTERISTICS OF THE HAND

Fingernails

a)   A well-formed, broad and full nail, with straight sides and a generally healthy appearance represents a well-balanced, down to earth and broad-minded individual. Expect this to go along with a well-grounded chart in which the elements are balanced, or with a strong Earth influence.

b)   Long, narrow nails on narrow fingers tend to go with a person who is not so physically strong as a) above, and who is more controlling and retentive. If the repressive nature is ingrained, the nails may even bend over at the top as they grow, looking like talons. Look in the chart for possibly over-controlling Saturn or retentive Pluto aspects.

c)   This classically beautiful oval shape to the fingernail is in tune with fine, long elegant fingers which belong to people who are not physical workers. These people are more likely to concern

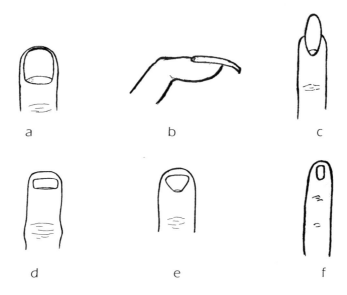

a   b   c

d   e   f

themselves with fine art and sensitive beauty. To see where these personal traits can be used to good advantage, look in the chart particularly at 2nd house (ruled by Venus and where a personal income may be generated), and 5th house (what is enjoyed and may be created).

d)   A broad, short nail is one which indicates that the critical faculties are coarsened by intolerance and quick temper. The flare-ups will be over and quickly forgotten (by them, if not by the more sensitive recipients!) This nail is a sign of a pugnacious nature. Look at Aries and Mars, particularly in combination with Saturn, Pluto or Uranus. For these fingernails in combination with square fingertips and 'obstinate' thumb joint (see Joints, figure.22), look for the intractability of Taurus. The outburst of fury may be a consequence of an element imbalance. (See chart example 3).

e)   A nail which is narrow at its base shows that there is some damage to the nervous/emotional system. These people are not emotionally calm; they probably worry and do not readily relax. There is a level of anxiety here, and these are the people who are most likely to bite their nails. Look in the chart for signs of nervous stress and exhaustion, and try to locate helpful outlets, maybe looking at the opposition point to a stressed midpoint planet.

f)   A very small nail, particularly on the Mercury (4th) finger is an indication of a critical nature. Criticism in this case may not be bad-tempered, but more of a particular attention to detail, and the person is most likely to be a stickler for perfection. Although the character may show as nit-picking, the fact is that the owner of this very small nail cannot tolerate sloppiness when it comes to detail. This person may do well in quality control, or documentation. Look for a strong Virgo influence here.

Vertical ridges, and flaking of the finger nails are suggestions of a stressed system, and possible nutritional imbalances. Look for stress lines on the palm, and for signs in the chart of emotional tensions and possible eating disorder.

A horizontal ridge growing up the finger nail can help to date the time of a shock to the system. The ridge is indented across the base of the nail at the time of the shock. The nail takes about six months to grow from base to tip. This can confirm the effect of a shock brought on by transits, particularly by Mars or Uranus.

A bulbous nail, rising up to a hump in the centre, suggests stress to or disease of the lungs. It could be a remnant of early TB, or be showing damage being suffered by the lungs through smoking.

Fingertip Patterns: Ridges

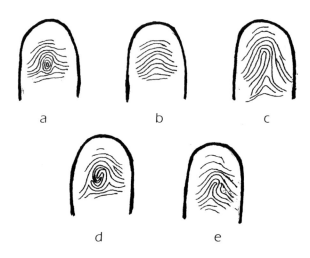

a   b   c

d   e

| a) | Whorl | Intensity, individualistic, content with own views. May well be self-employed as less adaptable to others. Look for Fixed influences. |

b)   Low Arch   Practical, reserved. Look for Earth influence.

c)   Looped Arch   Adaptable, open to the views of others. Look
                        for Mutable influences.

d)   Composite   Open to considering all sides of any matter,
                        interested in many things. Look for Air/Earth.

e)   Tented Arch   Sensitive, enthusiastic. Look for Fire influence.

Thumbs

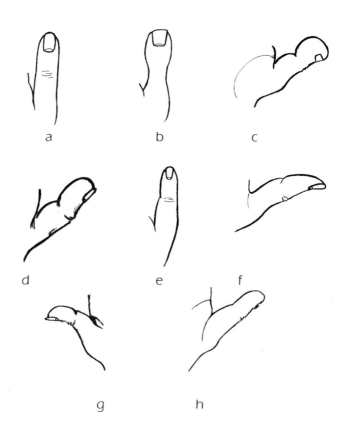

a   b   c

d   e   f

g   h

Examples of classic thumb shapes

The top, or 1st phalange of the thumb represents the will. The bottom, or 2nd phalange represents the capacity for logic. The joint between these two phalanges, if pronounced, shows determination, tenacity, or obstinacy, depending on the degree.

When the thumb is held at a wide angle from the hand, and when it is set low on the hand, it shows an adventurous, courageous nature. Conversely, when it is held folded into the hand, hidden away, it shows a fearful nature. Traditional oriental dancers can be observed holding their thumbs into the palm of the hand, in a gesture of submission.

a)   This thumb is well balanced; the will and the logic are evenly proportioned, with no abnormal emphasis. Expect to see a well-balanced chart to go with this example.

b)   This example shows a thumb with a pronounced 1st phalange, and a waisted 2nd phalange. In this case the will over-rides the logic. This person may push ahead without thinking first. Check the chart for a lack of Earth grounding, and look particularly at the condition of Mars and Uranus, which may point to a wilfulness, or Pluto for power. A weak Mercury may also point to a lack of logical thinking capacity.

c)   This thumb is what is classically referred to as 'the murderer's thumb'. It has a coarse, bulbous 1st phalange. When accompanied by a thin 2nd phalange (lack of logic) and a full, hard Mount of Venus, particularly on an elementary, unrefined hand, there may be the danger of a passionate wilfulness overwhelming the person, and violence ensuing. The planets Pluto, Mars and Saturn in bad combination may well be apparent. A badly-aspected or unaspected Moon may also add to the lack of a healthy connection to the emotions. Try to advise of times of especial danger, maybe Mars transits, when conflicts should be avoided.

d)   This thumb is short and solid, and should not be confused with example c). It looks as though it has been compressed, but is not coarsely bulbous. It belongs to someone who may have allowed their own will to be over-ridden by pressure from others, even a strong sense of duty to someone they feel responsible for. (See figure 13 – minor lines on the palm for family duty line). An over-strong nurturing instinct, perhaps excess Cancer influence, or too great an emphasis on the Water element can lead to the subjugation of will, and this repression will result at some stage in stress. The will and the logic of this thumb are not weak; they are compressed. Look for stress lines building up, and try to find outlets for personal expression.

e)   This thumb has a 1st phalange which is proportionately weak and small. It probably represents a low personal will, and the person may find it hard to push himself forward. If there is a stronger 2nd phalange, then he may learn to logic out a situation and develop a more normally balanced will. Look to see how the Sun, Mars, and the 2nd house of values are aspected in the chart, and try to find some area of expertise which could bring self-esteem and stimulate enthusiasm. Interest and enthusiasm can fire a person to develop determination. This person may even be seen to hold the thumb folded into the palm of the hand in a gesture of submission. Low self-esteem also shows as a 4th (Mercury) finger set lower on the palm than the other fingers.

f)   The 1st phalange of this thumb is long, generally flat, and pointed rather like an arrow. It is often seen on a thumb held confidently away from the palm. Expect the owners of this type of thumb to be very active, and often sporty. They tend to get things done and use their intellect to achieve what they set out to do. With a strong 2nd phalange, and a capacity for logical application, they can really succeed. Expect to see a good Jupiter-Mars combination in the chart.

g)   The flexibility of the joint between the 1st and 2nd phalanges of the thumb can be very noticeable. An extreme backward bend is genetically characteristic of some southern European nations, and if that is the case then there would be less significance than if this feature was to be seen in the hand of more northern nationalities. Some thumbs are restrained and inflexible, with no backward bend at all, even when pressed. At the other extreme, there are thumbs where the top phalange bends backwards so far, even forming a right angle, that it seems to be double-jointed. Example g) shows a flexible thumb. This characteristic can also extend to the fingers, where just the top joint may bend back, or the whole finger may bend backwards from the base joint, where it joins the palm. People with flexible joints are generally diplomatic. To some extent they may be said to 'bend over backwards' to keep other people happy (look at Libra and Venus), but it can suggest a lack of honesty, inasmuch as they may not tell the whole truth, but with the intention of keeping people content, 'adapting' one step too far, even to sycophancy in extreme cases. The chart may show signs of this trait, perhaps Jupiter is promising more than it can deliver. See also Mercury and Gemini for the honesty level, Libra for diplomacy.

h)   A pronounced basal joint of the thumb, where it joins the hand, is known as the 'angle of proficiency', and is commonly seen on the hands of craftsmen.

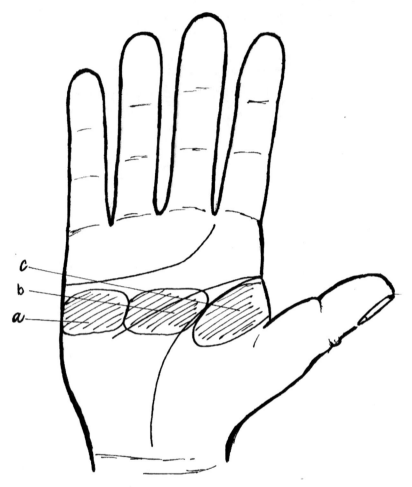

Figure 8 Mars areas on the palm

Mars Areas on the Hand

Figure 8 illustrates the areas of the palm which represent the energy of Mars. As is the case with all the Mounts on the hand (see Frontispiece for illustration), the fullness or hollowness of each area reflects the degree of emphasis in each case.

a)   This area suggests the degree of moral courage which exists. It is positioned under the Mercury finger on the Lunar side of the hand. Mercury is recognised as possibly being 'The Trickster', and a good, firm area here will add strength of moral character. It is sometimes called the Mars Negative area, less pro-active than Mars Positive (c).

b) This area shows strength of character. Feeling the thickness from the palm of the hand to the back of the hand will tell just how firm or hollow this area is. It sits between Mars Negative and Mars Positive, in the centre of the palm.

c) This area is known as Mars Positive. It shows the more pro-active reactions associated with Mars energy. When it is very full and bulbous it tells of a person with anger and aggression. The rest of the hand, and the chart itself, should be considered in order to gauge whether there is danger from what could become explosive aggression. The chart may well give information about the root cause of any anger, which can then be addressed. In conjunction with short, wide fingernails there may be temper outbursts, but there is a lot of energy here which should be given a safe outlet in order to be used positively.

Figure 9 Thumb mound on back of palm

Figure 9 illustrates the area on the back of the hand which shows the level of robustness of the person. When the thumb is held against the hand, this area will protrude to a greater or lesser degree – the greater the mound, the more robust the person physically.

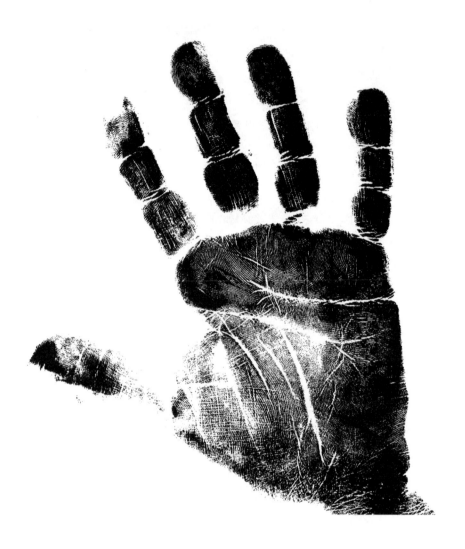

Figure 10 Lunar whorl handprint

The Loops on the Palm

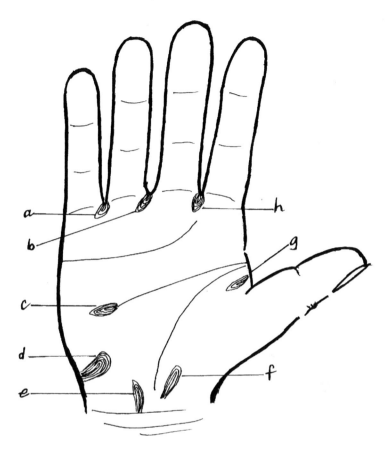

Figure 11 Loops on Palm

The skin ridge pattern on the palm of the hand can form whorls and loops. Wherever a whorl is seen there is an emphasis on that area, for example a whorl on the Mount of Luna suggests an imaginative, intuitive nature which may be appear in the natal chart as a 12th house or Neptune emphasis. (See figure 10 handprint and figure 14 chart). The basic loops are shown in figure11 :

a)   Loop of Humour. Look at Jupiter (jollity), Sun (vitality), and Mercury (communication).

b)   Loop of Serious Intent. This suggests a basic good intention, and a will to do the right and decent thing. Look at Saturn, Earth signs.

c)   Loop of Memory. This may be attached to the head line or on the Lunar Mount. The memory may be intellectual or instinctive. The Moon is regarded as representing memory.

d)   Loop of Nature. These people have a natural love of nature. Look for Earth element, Virgo and Taurus strengths.

e)   Loop of Poetic Inspiration. Look at Neptune.

f)   Loop of Music. Expect to see a harmonious aspect between Neptune and Venus. Neptune is the higher octave of Venus.

g)   Loop of Courage. This is in the physical Mars area. Expect to see Mars in an unhampered, prominent position, well grounded.

h)   Loop of Executive. This loop, between the 1st and 2nd fingers, is seen on the hands of people who have good executive or business ability and the ability to succeed in this sphere. Look at the aspects between and positions of Saturn and Jupiter.

Line Markings on the Hand

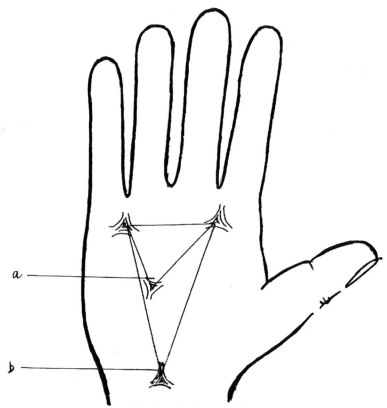

Figure 12 Triaxial Radii

Figure 12 shows the triaxial markings which appear in the skin ridges of the palm. Research has shown that when the markings form a close triangle (example a) then there is greater risk of heart disease than when the ridge patterns are more widely spaced (example b).

Markings on the hand do change. It is rare indeed to see a complete change of the major lines, although the character of the lines is subject to change, and they may extend or contract in length. They may become less or more clearly marked, and augmented by minor lines and markings in response to the conditions of life. It is the minor lines which are most subject to change, and which are most likely to illustrate dangers, fortunate and unfortunate occurrences, talents and

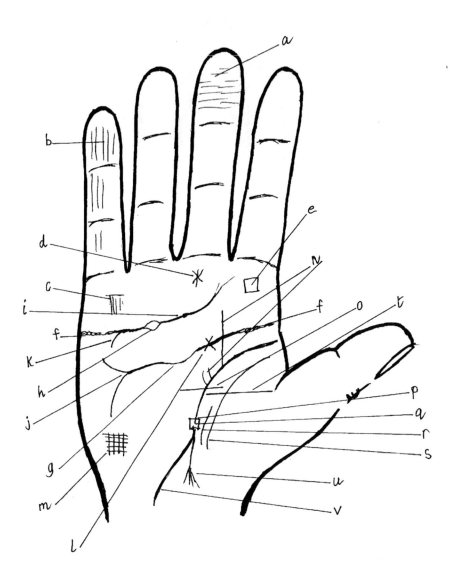

Figure 13 Line markings on the Hand

tendencies which may be well or only partly developed. Figure 13 illustrates a selection of line markings.

a)   Horizontal lines on the tips of the fingers are a sign of stress. The transiting aspects to the natal chart can help pinpoint where the stress is based.

b)   Vertical lines running up the fingers show that the tiredness is leading to exhaustion. Various planetary combinations may be involved – the Sun represents vitality, Mars the energy, Neptune the dissolving, Saturn restriction, or look at the nutrition.

c)   Samaritan lines. The classical marking is of three vertical lines topped by a horizontal line, on the Mount of Mercury, towards the Mount of Sun. Vertical lines in this position show an empathy for the fellow man and the human condition generally, and an urge to help heal the hurts of others. Samaritan lines are frequently found on the hands of therapeutic healers. In the natal chart, Chiron will probably be in aspect to the Sun and/or the personal planets. Expect to see some essential wounding to that person which has given an empathy for the pain of others. Neptune may also be indicating sympathy, some spirituality, but possibly idealism.

d)   The Star. When a star is marked on one of the Mounts of the palm it is usually regarded as positive, but when it is on one of the main lines it is interpreted in the same way as a cross (see I below).

e)   The Square. On the Mount of Jupiter, a square is known as 'the teacher's square'. Jupiter is concerned with teaching, as Saturn is concerned with being the authority. Jupiter and the 9th house are often prominent in the charts of natural teachers. If the lines are faintly marked, then perhaps the chart will show the teaching ability, but it may not have been developed.

f)   Chained lines. Chaining in the formation of the main lines, particularly the Life or Heart line, suggests an unsettled beginning to life. As the line becomes clearer and more positive in its progression, so the insecurities are seen to be overcome. A look at the first houses of the chart, to assess early experience; the Moon, and the 4th house to see the home conditions; may give the right information.

g)   Main lines drooping. If the main line droops for a period of its progress, it indicates a period of low vitality or suffering in the sphere represented by that line. For example, a drooping section during the course of the Head line represents a period of depression. The whole condition of the Head line will tell if the person is a natural, long-term depressive, but a drooping section probably ties up with stressful transits of the outer planets, or Saturn. (See section on depression.)

h)   Island. Where a main line splits and rejoins to form an island it marks a place of stress, often illness, and the area of the hand is significant. On either the Heart line or Head line, an island under the 3rd finger indicates eye trouble, under the Saturn finger ear trouble.

i)   Spot. A spot marking on one of the main lines is a bad indication of a time of difficulty, maybe shock.

j)   Dividing Line. Where one of the main lines divides, it is a sign that the matters concerned with that line go in two directions at once. For example, if the Head line divides towards its end, under the Finger of Mercury, with one line rising up towards Mercury and the other one curving down into the Mount of Lunar, then this is known as the 'writer's fork'. The line curving into the Mount of Lunar shows a creativity and imagination. The line rising towards Mercury gives a business sense. The implication is that this person has the ability to use his creative gift to make money.

k)   Dropping line. Any line which drops down from a major line suggests a time of sadness or disappointment. For instance, a line dropping down from the Heart line, suggests a major disappointment in love. A whole selection of planetary geometry may be active here: Saturn in hard aspect to Venus, maybe an enlightening Uranus transit giving quite a shock to the system, following a period of Neptune to Venus idealism or self-deception. The whole chart will need to be considered, because the response to a situation will vary from person to person.

l)   Cross. A cross on one of the lines is regarded as a malefic event. Look at danger signs in the horoscope.

m)   Grille. A cross-hatching of fine lines on the palm suggest a health breakdown in some area. On the Lunar Mount, look for a urinary problem.

n)   Rising Lines. These are good lines, signifying times of effort and achievement. For instance, a line rising from the Life line ties up with a period of great effort which has led to some personal betterment or accomplishment. One planetary example would be Jupiter transiting natal Pluto where – depending on all the other details of the chart – a great effort would be likely to bring success. Quick overnight success, of course, does tend to follow a period of hard work. If Saturn's sustainability is the first part of the transiting picture, followed by Jupiter's good fortune, then the success brought by Jupiter, after the efforts of Saturn, is much more probable.

o)   Opposition Line. A line cutting through the Life line suggests that there is opposition at that point, probably from within the family. Perhaps there is a Pluto opposition (to Mercury or Moon?), suggesting that someone is trying to manipulate you to control what you do to suit their own ends.

p)   Broken Line. A break in the line is a break in the passage of that particular energy. For instance, a break in the Life line may appear as a gap, with the line recommencing in the same direction, or the line may recommence further out into the palm of the hand, or further in on the Mount of Venus, closer to the thumb. Each of these breaks indicates a change in the life pattern. When the line recommences further out, into the palm, it suggests that the change will involve a broadening of horizons. Where it recommences further into the Mount of Venus, it suggests that in some way the new period of life will be more restricted. Perhaps the person will have some physical restriction, or they may choose to limit their sphere of activity. The break may be because of an injury or illness, but that is not essentially so. Signs of protection during this break are shown in q) and r) below. Neptune may encourage someone to retreat, in which case expect the line to move closer to the thumb. Uranus may make a sudden change. Jupiter may expand experience, in which case expect the line to continue further out into the palm of the hand.

q)   Square. A square on one of the lines is a sign of protection. It is often seen to span a break in a line, and acts as a bridge which carries the passage of the line safely through the danger period.

r)   Protection Line. This line runs alongside the main line, and acts as a back-up to cover the danger period suggestion by the break in or fading of the line. It acts as a 'helping angel' to support the person through a difficult time.

s)   Companion Line. This is a line which runs in parallel with the main Life line. It is said to represent a supporting companion. I have seen this line on the hand of someone whose Life line held close to the thumb, and the thumb held close to the hand. The Companion line had run in parallel to the Life line for much of its passage, then it joined the Life line, and did not continue. From that point the Life line became much weaker. The situation it represented was that there had been a secret committed love, which could not be actualised because of personal responsibilities. The closely held thumb, and the Life line tight on the Mount of Venus suggested that this person did not have the courage to stand firm and take what she wanted. Eventually the family responsibilities diminished, and the lovers came together, but at that point the partner died, and the owner of this palm had a breakdown. As time went on, the Life line grew stronger and formed a new branch, which reached out into the palm. The main Life line remained close to the thumb, which indicated the innate lack of courage in her nature although she was expanding her life. The Companion Line faded to a very faint one. Some people experience this Companion Line as a feeling that they are supported on a spiritual level, if not in a worldly way. The nature of the person may reflect the sort of support felt.

t)   Duty Line. This line illustrates a sense of duty, particularly to the family. Saturn represents responsibility. The 4th and 10th house axis represents the parents.

u)   Frayed End. When one of the major lines frays at the end it is an indication of fading energy in that sphere. It could be mental or physical. Neptune may be implicated here. It would be seen as a danger signal which may be improved with attention to the health, life conditions or nutrition.

v)   The illustrated example shows the frayed end of the original Life line (u), with a new, well marked extension of this line (v) reaching out into the palm. This shows that one way of life has faded out to be replaced by another, with broader horizons. This could represent emigration to a new life.

Transits

Changes seen on the hand generally correlate to transits to the natal chart. Transits by planets from Mars outwards can be most noticeable in their effect, but look also to solar arc and secondary progression conjunctions and oppositions for the effects of the faster-moving personal planets. Tight orbs, down to 1 degree, should be used when considering solar arcs and secondary progressions.

Just as any transiting planet has a period of time when it is approaching the conjunction or aspect, so there is a built-up within the person. If this is producing tension, mental or emotional imbalance, then the hand will reflect it through signals such as excess fine stress lines, skin ridges breaking down, nails ridged or flaking, or even the main lines fading. These are alarm signals to lead you to look for the cause of the imbalance, and for a possible approaching transit to work towards and prepare for. Awareness of an approaching transit gives the opportunity to question what area of life may be affected, and should give a better chance for the transit to be experienced positively.

For example, I saw a client whose natal chart showed her to be unstable and overwhelmed by sensation. At the time of our consultation Saturn was transiting through her 12th house. She was feeling fearful and uncertain of her future, unsuccessful and emotionally very needy. Her handprints showed the 1st and 4th fingers curving in at their tops towards the middle two fingers, a classic sign of emotional dependency (see Fig 24 page 61, text page 60). During this time she was able to reflect on her life, and to realise that her emotional dependency had held her back from maturing fully as a person. When Saturn crossed her Ascendant she made a determined effort to take responsibility for herself. She began a colour therapy art course, and the excitement which she felt from the colour vibrations and from the creative process went a long way to satisfy her need for sensation. She became a more mature person. Within a year and a half her fingers changed. They no longer curved, but were standing confidently straight and well spaced. The compounding over many years of emotional instability and dependency had been recognised, and although these traits would remain as a tendency in her character, by being helped to understand the dynamic of her present condition and potential, she had been able to make full use of Saturn's 12th house transit, and its passage across her Ascendant.

Long-term conditions are often brought to a head by significant Jupiter or Saturn transits. Each of these planets has a connection with the law and justice, with bringing life back into proper balance. Jupiter trine Uranus may bring a lucky opportunity, sometimes to be freed from an oppressive situation, which could have shown in the hands as frustration or stress lines. Saturn transits bring an opportunity, or a pressing need to change the very structure of how the life is being lived and to resolve issues that may have been lurking in the background for a while.

The effect of any transit can depend on what preparation has been made for it. If the way life is structured is well balanced, and whatever may have been set up at the time of a previous Saturn transit is working well, then changes may not be called for. The hand will not show any build up of imbalance, and the transit may pass without much noticeable effect.

When a transit activates a significant configuration in the chart, such as a T-square, the effect can be dynamic. Even a Mars transit, which passes fairly quickly, may inject enough energy to act as a catalyst and to inflame a situation enough to demand attention.

Some transits do appear to have immediate effect although there will undoubtedly have been some kind of build-up: an undiagnosed illness that seems to suddenly surface, or an accident that may in fact follow a period of recklessness or carelessness, or repressed energy.

Timing on the Hand

Traditionally there has been a theory that the timing of major events is marked at certain distances along the 3 major lines. Certainly the markings on the major lines are significant, but measuring the timing can be confusing. Some hands show a short Life Line, even though the life itself may prove to be long in years. That short line may or may not be augmented by joining with another line later, but should not be taken to predict a very short life. Dividing a line such as this into years can make it difficult to determine the exact timing of an incident. Generally, an event at 30 years of age will appear as a mark approximately one third of the distance from the beginning of the Life Line – but if the line later grows an extension, then accurately assessing a time scale can be difficult.

The marks and lines on the main lines which act as indications of events tend to build up fairly gradually, and they can fade after the event. The degree to which these marks remain etched on the hand is an indication of how deep and lasting their effect has been. Likewise, the signs of imbalance which build up in the period approaching a transit should fade after its passing. If the stress signals remain, and the requirements of the transit have been ignored or suppressed, then a future transit could have a more dramatic effect..

Moon-Saturn

There are orbital connections between the Moon and Saturn. The Moon's orbit in days is equal to Saturn's orbit in years, and therefore one secondary progressed Moon orbit equals one transiting Saturn orbit. Both Moon and Saturn are concerned with security. There is a polarity in the chart, as each rules the sign in opposition to the other.

As ruler of Cancer, the Moon's connection with emotional security and mothering is recognised. If the Moon's position is not strong, if it is negatively aspected by being overpowered by other planets, such as a hard aspect from Saturn making for a degree of repressive control or inhibition, then insecurity is suggested. When a person is feeling insecure, the fingers may be held closely together and curved into the palm, fearful of standing straight and spreading wide. The Cancer/Capricorn polarity may then come into play, and the person looks to Capricornian activity – work, property, structure, material possession rather than emotional involvement. If the need for security is not met by a comforting and loving family, then it may be looked for in the fabric of the home itself, the property. Fear of loss may even lead to the person holding on too tightly, apparently treating their family as their own property. Some foundation must be sought, whether from home or house. The emotions are by nature fluctuating, and without a firm foundation can be painful and even dangerous.

This matter of looking to the opposite sign to counteract weaknesses in one sign can operate throughout the chart. It also comes into play when there is a midpoint planet under stress; for example, with a T-square, that is where two planets are in opposition to each other, with a third planet at a 90 degree angle to the opposing planets. The midpoint planet, at the apex point of the right-angle triangle, is at a stress point, and a stress outlet may be achieved by looking at the point on the chart circle opposite the apex (stressed) planet.

Changing Lines – An Individual Example

This example of a major change to one of the main lines on the palm reflects the passage of Saturn in relation to the natal chart.

The birth chart itself (figure 14) shows a Libran Ascendant, with the chart ruler, Venus, in its own sign and conjunct the Ascendant. Mars also conjuncts Venus and the Ascendant, and Neptune is also widely conjunct Mars and Venus. At first glance this appears lovely, but the planets are hidden away in the 12th house, and are subject to an

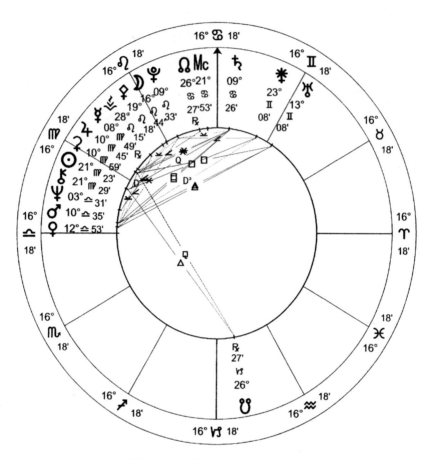

Figure 14 Example birth chart

approaching square by Saturn. Saturn is the highest planet in the chart, and is thus strongly placed.

In a female chart particularly, Saturn's square to Venus is generally undermining to the self-esteem and the confidence in oneself as a woman. It could have brought into the life the experience of controlling relationships. In this chart, with the leading and following planets being Uranus and Venus in a trine to each other, the controlling would probably have caused frustration and a tendency to break away. Saturn squaring the Venus-Mars conjunction in the 12th house would have led to hidden suffering and repressed anger, in spite of the charming Libran Ascendant.

When Saturn has such a powerful position, then it is to be

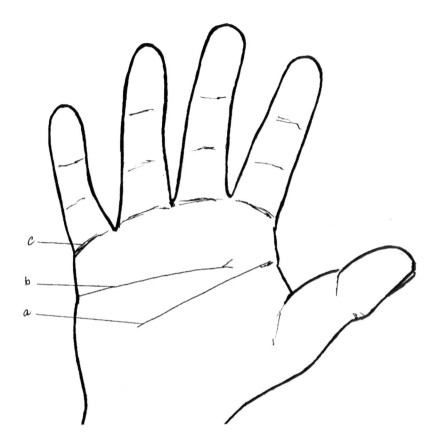

Figure 15 Left hand

expected that any major transits it makes to its own natal position, and consequently here to Venus and Mars, will have a deep effect. The natal configuration will be activated and brought to the forefront of life, asking to be attended to and controlled or restructured in some way.

The left hand, illustrated in figure 15 illustrates a straight, practical Head line (a) and a Heart line which is also straight and biased towards the Head line (b) rather than curving up towards the fingers. The 4th finger, the Mercury finger, is set considerably lower than the other fingers (c). These details are very much in line with the effect of Saturn in the natal chart. The affairs of the heart are contained by the practicality of the straight line. The romanticism of the Neptune, Mars-Venus combination is repressed. The low-set 4th finger shows the effect on the self-esteem.

Looking at the right hand (figure 16), the Heart line has charted the effect of Saturn's transits. It had developed a healthy curve, right up to the inner edge of the Jupiter Mount (d). The Head line split into a Writer's Fork (e), with a branch leading into the Lunar area. In this way the creative energies and intuition shown in this chart were given the opportunity to develop.

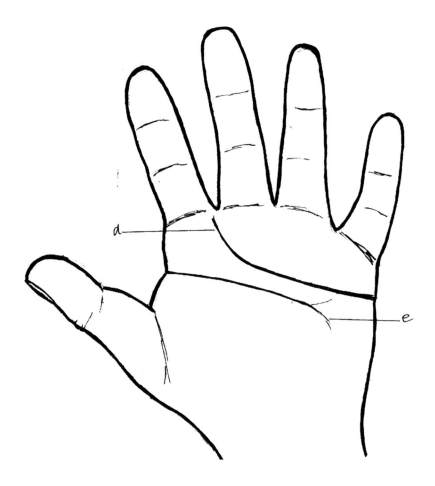

Figure 16 Right hand

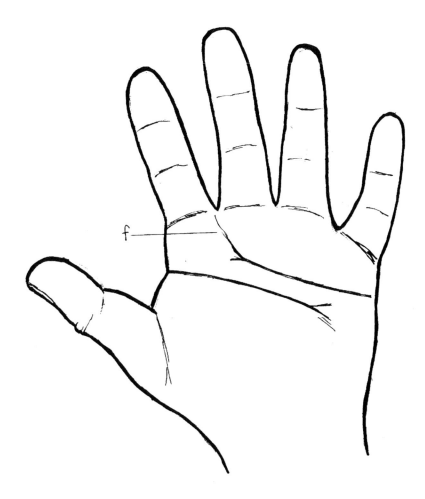

Figure 17 Saturn Transit

Saturn transits brought changes. At the time of the 'mid-life crisis', when Saturn opposed its natal position, the whole natal configuration was activated. One consequence was divorce, and the resultant shrinking back of the Heart line, right back down to the Head line (see figure 17). During the following years the Heart line reformed to its former course, but its condition was much fainter (f).

Then came the second Saturn Return. Saturn reinforced its natal influence. There was an experience which brought the natal condition very prominently into the life. As Saturn transits call for some restructuring, and as the second Saturn Return so often prompts unnecessary burdens to be left behind, so some changes could be expected here. The Heart line at this time now retracted completely back to match that on the left hand – a shrinking back to the natal state.

A year or two after the Saturn Return, there was a delightful major configuration of planets. Transiting Neptune, in the 5th house, came to form a grand trine with the natal Venus-Uranus trine. This could easily lead an astrologer to look for a romantic love experience, and an expectation that the Heart line would extend once more.

What actually happened under this grand trine influence was indicated by the Heart line on the right hand. It did not extend back to its former curve up to the fingers. It did actually curve a little upwards, but remained essentially rather short. The exciting, romantic vibrations of the Neptune-Venus-Uranus grand trine were actually experienced through music and colour, which were felt right through the body as ecstatic beautiful vibrations. This is one example which should caution the astrologer not to jump to any conclusions about what seems to be an inevitable consequence of transits, but to consider the true dynamic of the energies, and to study the effect on the lines and condition of the hands.

Lines on the Hand – The Bracelets

Forecasting when someone will become a parent is not absolutely predictable; so much depends on the dynamic of the experience, how it affects the potential parent. The birth of each child can be experienced differently on psychological and physical levels. For instance, when a child is born under a Pluto transit to the natal Sun in the chart of the mother, the birth may be experienced as a complete physical and psychological transformation; or when Saturn is crossing the Ascendant the parent may experience a great sense of taking on a new responsibility.

Jupiter in the 5th house may make the birth feel like a lucky and optimistic satisfaction of the creative urge. The natal 5th house, the Sun and Leo, may give a suggestion of the creative potential.

The Bracelets are a group of lines at the base of the hand, on the wrist, and their condition shows whether there is a danger of difficulty in childbirth. It does not necessarily preclude bearing children; perhaps the birth itself may be complicated.

The Bracelets are made up of three lines running across the wrist. The lines themselves are wider than the lines on the palm, and usually appear somewhat chained. When there are three complete and well-formed lines (figure 18a) then there are likely to be no problems with childbirth, and a good general state of health is suggested. If the top line rises up into the palm of the hand (figure 18b) then there could potentially be problems with childbirth, and special care and attention to health should be given. An awareness of this condition need not instil fear; to be vigilant about health care and birthing conditions can avoid trouble.

Sometimes the lines of the Bracelets are broken and do not run right across the wrist. This is believed to represent a lack of robust health. Perhaps Mars or the Sun are receiving debilitating transits or aspects.

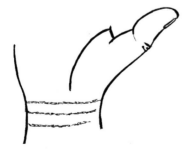

Figure 18a

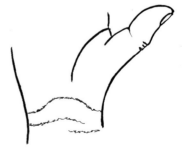

Figure 18b

Fingers and Hands – 3 Divisions

The fingers are made up of three sections, or phalanges. Just as each section of the finger has its own sphere of influence, so does each third of the hand, and they run in parallel with each other. Figure 19 illustrates how the three finger sections correspond to the three hand sections.

a)   Of the fingers, the top, or 1st, phalange relates to mental activity. When looking at the whole hand, the finger section is regarded as the top section.

b)   The middle, or 2nd, phalange of the finger relates to the practical application of a person's abilities, to the employment and likely achievement. The section of the hand from the Mount of Jupiter on one side to the Mount of Mercury on the other, beneath the fingers and above the Mount of Venus, across the hand's whole width, represents the 2nd section.

c)   The bottom, or 3rd, phalange relates to material and physical matters. The lower section of the hand, from the Mount of Venus to the base, and across the hand's width, represents the 3rd section.

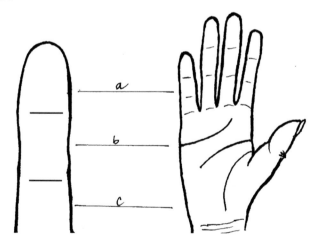

Figure 19 Finger and Hand divisions

The relative length, width and fullness, coarseness or flabbiness, reflect the balance of strength of each division. If, for example, a hand is broad and coarsely full at the base, with puffy basal, 3rd, phalanges to the fingers, but the 2nd, middle, sections are weaker and narrower, then there is a lack of balance. It is less likely that this person will achieve worldly success. A look at the chart may also show if there is danger from the base areas, or if there is just a self-indulgent laziness, with a baseness of attitude.

Basic Fingertip Shapes

See figure 20 for diagrams.

a)   Square tip. This shows a practical nature.

b)   Spatulate tip. The tip of this finger spreads out at the top, wide and firm. These are the people who can do the very finest of craft work. It is often seen in conjunction with the 'angle of proficiency', which is a pronounced joint at the base of the thumb, at the point where it joins the hand.

c)   Round tip. These people are generally sensitive and not extreme. Whether or not they can apply their artistic ability depends upon the level of practicality. Look at the 2nd phalange.

d)   Pointed tip. The tip which comes to a point shows an impractical nature, where the love of beauty may rule above the urge to work.

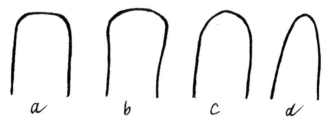

Figure 20 Four basic fingertip shapes

Figure 21 illustrates what is known as a Droplet, which can be seen on the 1st phalange of any or all of the fingers. When viewed from the side, the appearance of the pronounced flesh of the tip looks as if it forms a droplet. Owners of this characteristic have a very sensitive touch, and can be very tactile.

Figure 21 Droplets

The Joints of the Fingers

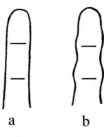

a   b

Figure 22 Joints

The character of the joints of the fingers illustrates the mode of thinking. Smooth jointed fingers (figure 22a) represent a mind which takes information in directly, even intuitively. Short-fingered people can think so quickly that they may become impatient with those who are more slow and thoughtful. Long-fingered people are generally more patient and considerate. Figure 22b illustrates a finger with knotty joints. The knots of the fingers seem to slow down thought. They belong to those who analyse and consider the information presented, before accepting it, and who may be considered as ponderous. These people like to have their thoughts in a good mental order. These knotty fingers are often seen on the philosophical type of person, who may have a strong Sagittarian outlook.

Knotty, swollen joints can also be a symptom of a rheumatic, arthritic illness. This condition is seen in the natal chart as relating to Saturn. Saturn likes to restrict, control, structure and generally organise. When applied to the mental process, the person feels the need to control and order their thoughts and feelings. The physiological correspondence is a body structure – the bones, which are so over-contained that the joints become inflexible and may become inflamed as a reaction.

RELATIONSHIPS
The Need for Space

Achieving the most comfortable degree of space within a personal relationship, work situation, or any partnership, can be a difficult balancing act. Quite explosive stress can build up in a person who feels pressure to fit into a pattern of relationship which is at odds with his own needs. Many relationships fail because a person cannot function fully when expectation becomes too demanding. This is the case whether someone needs to have his own space in order to feel comfortable, or whether he feels secure only when he is with someone else all day and every day.

A need for space within a close relationship is a very Aquarian trait. The most likely planetary aspects to suggest this would probably involve Uranus aspects to Venus or Moon. The Air signs, Gemini, Libra and Aquarius, are often strongly prominent. Whenever the Moon is posited in an Air sign then that person is more able to be emotionally detached, even in the case of Libra, the sign of balance and relationship. Sagittarius also demands freedom, because it is motivated to follow its own quest, and that motivation may over-ride any other. When the eastern side of the chart is the one most heavily occupied, particularly by the personal planets, then assume that personal relationship is not an over-riding need to that person. Those with most emphasis on the Ascendant side of the natal chart tend to be more independent.

Venus is always to be considered in relationship and attraction. It rules Libra and the 7th house. Libra, the Scales, always tries to achieve a balance and harmony, and needs someone on the other side of the scales in order to achieve that balance. The Libran desire to achieve harmony and give the appearance that all is well can actually cover a manipulative trait. There can be a tendency to organise or manipulate a person or situation, in a charming way, to achieve the appearance of harmony and balance – rather like an iron fist in a velvet glove. The fact is that Libra is an Air sign, and sometimes the way to achieve a harmonious and pleasant relationship may not be through unconditional love, although it may shock the Libran to consider this as a possibility.

The 7th house, being opposite to, and in polarity with, the 1st house of self, indicates personal or business, contracted partnerships. It is said to also represent 'the open enemy', as opposed to 'the secret enemy' of the 12th house. With Aquarius on the cusp of the 7th house, or Uranus placed in that house, there is an immediate suggestion of sudden changes within partnership. This can be the result of not achieving the right balance of independence to dependence.

The very fact that Uranus or Aquarius occupy the 7th house shows that the person needs to experience space and personal freedom within partnership. When the suggestion of disrupted relationships shows itself in the 7th house of a chart, consider the possibility of psychological projection. Unconsciously, the person may choose or be attracted to a partner who will provide the situation, and who may be blamed for it. It could well be that it is the partner who disrupts the relationship. Projection shows up in the opposing sign, the other extreme, of that polarity. Matters of one house can be readily cast into the opposite house, and in the case of the 1st house, the house of self, it is the 7th house, the house of the partner, where the scenario can work out without seeming to reflect on the behaviour of the person himself. Thus it maintains appearances, an Ascendant and 1st house matter.

Figure 23 shows a hand of a person needing personal space. The main feature of this hand is that the 2nd and 3rd fingers lean away from each other at the tips. This is the most common signature of someone who needs his own space. The separation of the fingers may extend right down the length of the finger, to the base. The thumb is probably held at a confident and independent angle, away from the palm.

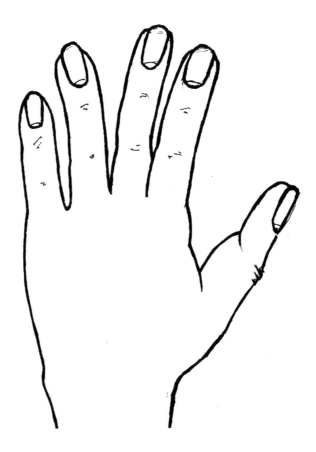

Figure 23 Needing space

Dependency

When the houses on the western side of the chart are heavily occupied by the personal planets, then expect that person to naturally get involved with other people, and to need personal interaction. This is not the same as emotional dependency on a one-to-one relationship. If, for instance, there is a strong Gemini influence, the social contact may actually be with many people and on a more casual or shallow level. Astrological suggestions of emotional dependency will be seen by the condition of the natal Moon, Saturn and the Water element signs in particular.

Of the Water signs, Cancer is the most clingy, and may be quite circumspect in the way it manipulates a situation in order to achieve emotional security. Cancer's ruler, the Moon, will give much information about the emotional conditioning. In hard aspect with Saturn there will be issues of emotional insecurity. This can result in a fear of one's own feelings, with consequent behaviours of avoidance. A person afraid of his own feelings may appear to be cold and unfeeling, and such may be the case when the Moon, ruler of Cancer, is posited in Capricorn, its opposing Sign, under the influence of Saturn. Saturn can restrict and control the Moon's fluctuating emotions in quite a lonely and depressing way. The Moon/Saturn insecurity can lead someone to cling closely to their family for support throughout the whole lifespan. Sometimes a person's fear can bring about a habitual state of anxiety; the Moon reflects habits.

A strong Scorpio or Pluto influence, particularly to the Moon or Venus, brings with it an intense and overpowering emotion, and a great difficulty in letting go. This can tie a person into a psychological dependency, because he cannot release the partner.

In the case of Pisces, the third Water element sign, the dependency may be due to a need for martyrdom. It can give the face of unconditional love. Bear in mind that the 'unconditional love' may be a way of avoiding having to take responsibility for one's own life, and of

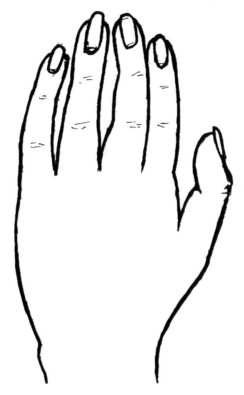

Figure 24 Dependency

actually depending on another person to make the decisions. After all if, on the face of it, one loves someone or depends on them to such a self-sacrificial degree, then one is not free to stand alone, and is in effect a dependent.

Figure 24 illustrates emotional dependency. The thumb is likely to be held close to the hand, showing a lack of personal courage, but the main feature of this hand is to be seen in the 2nd and 3rd fingers. They lean closely towards each other at the tip. The leaning inwards may extend to the whole set of fingers, leaning towards and clinging to each other at the tips.

MONEY

Attitude to Money

Feelings can run high where money is concerned, and this raises the question of what money actually represents. What a person puts a value on, what he aims to achieve, and the energy he has available to put into the effort, should all be illustrated by the natal chart. The chart may suggest whether someone is likely to have money difficulties, whether a fortune may be inherited or earned, and the attitude that person has to money.

The primary houses to be considered would be the 2nd, the house of values and personal income, and the 8th, the house of other people's money, of banks, and finance brought to a person through someone else, including inheritance.

The sign on the cusp of the 2nd house gives a first indication of the attitude to money and income, tempered by all the planetary aspects. Taurus is the natural ruling sign of the 2nd house, and Taurus is attuned to physical comfort and security, matters which in our society usually require money to achieve. Its ruling planet is Venus, which also rules Libra, the Scales – the balance. The £ sign developed over the years from the letter L, the initial letter of the Latin word 'libra', meaning a pound of money weighed on a balance scale. Libra is natural ruler of the 7th house, that of contracted partnership. The partnership may be personal, as a marriage partner, or it may be a business partnership. Love and Money are closely associated. Very many partnerships fail when money worries arise. A common, though often denied, scenario is: "You withdraw your love from me, so I withdraw my money from you", or, from the other side, "You refuse me physical support, so I refuse you love".

When the Moon is natally posited in the 2nd house, then that person is likely to value money as a way of achieving emotional security. With Saturn in the 2nd house, this ruler of the sign in polarity with the

Moon's sign (Cancer-Capricorn), may cause a feeling of insecurity regarding money, as if there will never be enough. People with this placement are likely to feel that they must keep working to get money, to alleviate their fear of physical insecurity. They can appear to be mean and withholding.

Figure 25 shows a hand which we could call mean. It gives the impression of tight-fistedness. The fingers are held closely together (a),

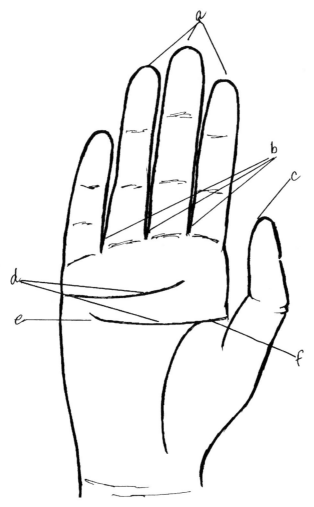

Figure 25 A 'mean' hand

and are joined closely at the base (b). The thumb is held in, close to the hand (c). The Heart and Head lines are running in straight lines across the hand, rather than curving. Emotions have not swayed them from their straight courses (d), suggesting a cooler, more practical outlook, and the Head line is more likely to rise at its end (e), under the Mercury finger, showing a talent for business, or to be short and straight. In this example, the Life line clings to the Head line for the first part of its passage (f), which illustrates an insecurity in the early part of life. These are all symptoms of a meanness based on a basic insecurity.

When there are opposition aspects between 2nd and 8th houses, then there could be other issues to look into. The 8th house is ruled naturally by Pluto, so sex and manipulative behaviour may come into the equation here. A heavily tenanted 8th house could suggest someone who uses his or her sexual favours to achieve the power he or she feels is needed, and this power may be secured through the possession of money.

Venus, as it is concerned with love, money and attraction, and ruling the 2nd house, must always be one of the first planets to consider. If it receives a hard aspect from Saturn, then there may well be an undermining of that person's self esteem. Venus rules the 2nd house of the value system, and represents attraction; that is, what one attracts and how attractive one feels. The hard aspects from Saturn restrict the sense of feeling attractive and valuable. Saturn to Venus aspects also coincide with a possible money shortage. For example, when Saturn transits the natal Venus then there is often a period of hard work for apparently little money, and also of coldness and possible break-up of a love relationship. A partnership formed under this combination may have a security aspect to it, and a sense of responsibility.

Figure 26 illustrates a hand which shows a nature much more open with money. Here you would expect to see spaces at the base of the fingers (a), with the fingers standing away from each other in an

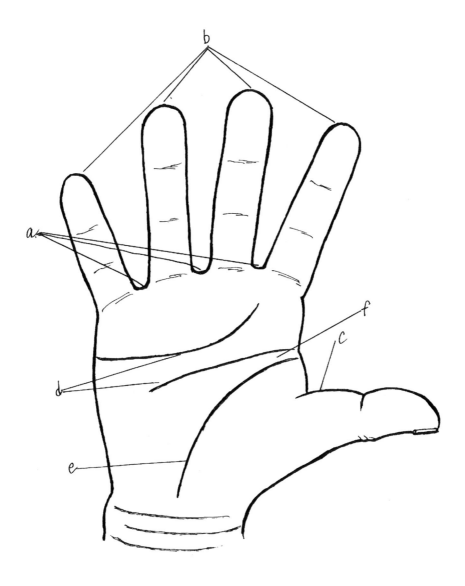

Figure 26 An 'open' hand

open-handed way (b), a thumb which is confidently held away from the hand (c), main lines curved rather than straight (d). You would expect to see a Life line reaching out across the palm (e), and starting independent of the Head line, with a space between the Head and Life lines at their beginning (f). These feelings of independence and confidence can help to free a person from an urge to accumulate wealth in order to feel supported. There are several different characteristics which can lead to someone not holding on to money:

a)   An Aquarian influence gives a more detached and independent outlook, more humanitarian and less concerned with individual worldly possession. Uranus in the 2nd house may suggest sudden changes or disruptions in the financial fortune, or unusual and innovative ways of acquiring money.

b)   Pisces on the cusp of the 2nd house, or Neptune within it can mean that the person does not quite get a grip of money, is rather vague about it, and finds that it just disappears. It can mean that values are spiritual rather than material, or that practical thought is clouded.

c)   Jupiter and Sagittarius can manifest, depending always on the aspects, as a gambler. This is sometimes seen in a Jupiter-Neptune combination, where the person takes a risk for an unachievable dream; Sagittarius is on a quest, and Jupiter is over-optimistic about the outcome. Jupiter-Venus, particularly in trine to each other from the 2nd house, is likely to show as someone who enjoys spending money on themselves indulgently, and often for show. Jupiter-Pluto in aspect, along with aspecting to the natal Sun, is often seen in people who can achieve great personal success and money from tremendous effort. It is common in the charts of leading sportsmen. The Sagittarian, or Jupiter, type of character may also carry a strong 9th house influence, where the philosophy is all-important. The quest to be followed over-rides any earthly materialism, and money is not the God. Expect to see knotty joints to the fingers with this sort of mindset. Jupiter is the optimist, but this planet does not always bring the expected good fortune. It is, after all, the Thunderbolt planet, one of the law and justice planets. Whereas Saturn is considered to be lord of karmic law, strict retribution, Jupiter may be thought of as representing a more worldly legal system, and transits involving Jupiter can bring a crashing down of over-inflated expectation, feeling much like a thunderbolt to the recipient.

Health

Food

Taurus, natural ruling sign of the 2nd house, is concerned with physical, sensual pleasure and security. Venus, its ruling planet, is also concerned with comfort and pleasure. Food, and what it represents, is a major part of this picture. Venus speaks of sweet foods, Jupiter of rich foods and an excess . As the ruling planet of Libra, Venus also affects concerns of balance. Whether due to sugar imbalance, or hormonal disturbances, stress signs on the fine lines of the hand may give pointers to dietary problems.

One of the four main asteroids, Ceres, is also concerned with food. Ceres is goddess of the harvest, of cereals, and illustrates nurturing, which includes feeding, particularly in the early days of life. Feeding is the very first experience of nurturing the new-born child receives. In strong aspect with Jupiter there may be an excess of nourishment, or of food production, whereas when Ceres is in hard aspect with Saturn there could be some restriction or controlling of food intake. Figure 27 illustrates a hand which shows signs of food excess.

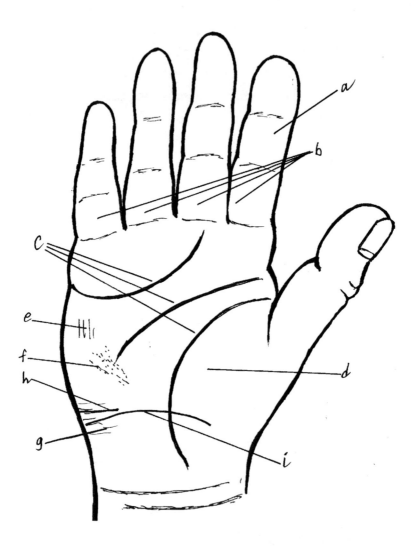

Figure 27 Excess Food

a)   A large and heavy 1st (Jupiter) finger can go with a large appetite.

b)   The basal phalanges of the fingers are podgy and full. If this podginess has extended to the backs of the fingers, then obesity is probably a long standing condition.

c)   The main lines of the hand are probably curved, suggesting a feeling nature.

d)   The Mount of Venus is full and fleshy, showing sensual energy.

e)   The stress lines running vertically at the top of the Mount of Luna, under the Mercury finger and the Heart line, are indicating a build-up of acid, possibly caused by stress, which could lead to an arthritic condition, or calcification. A control on the diet, with less acid intake, could help.

f)   Breaking up of the skin ridge pattern on the Mount of Lunar suggests that the body is reacting to stress on the digestive system, probably an overload of one sort or another, possibly toxin or alcohol.

g)   Fine lines on the outside of the Mount of Lunar can show food sensitivities.

h)   A line running in from the percussion edge of the hand and cutting into the Mount of Lunar is known as an Allergy line. This line is found on the hand of people who have some food intolerance.

i)   The Via Lascivia line, associated with addiction.

In a relatively short space of time we have been subjected to a whole range of substances in our environment and our diet, and our bodies may not have adapted completely, particularly to toxins. This causes problems to a sensitive system.

A person may eat some item of food for years without any apparent problem, only to eventually find that the body has built up a sensitivity to it and will no longer tolerate it. This reaction typically shows itself in early to middle adult life, but it can happen at any stage. The body can then no longer absorb this substance and reacts to it as if it were a poison, and so a reaction takes place. Symptoms can include tiredness, and itchy skin – trying to rid the body of the toxin. Behavioural problems have also been blamed on chemical food additives. A major symptom which can then develop is a craving for the guilty substance, or foodstuff, with withdrawal symptoms including depression. The body feels an addiction to the poison.

This addictive reaction can be shown in the hand by an extension of the Allergy line into a full-blown Via Lascivia line (i). The line runs from the Mount of Lunar at one end and into the Mount of Venus at the other, and indicates that the sensual pleasures of the Mount of Venus have become an addiction. This line used to be associated with alcoholism and low living, hence the term Via Lascivia – lascivious living. When food sensitivity, or abnormal reaction to substance, becomes addiction, then alcoholism is understandable as one of the most easily recognisable examples of this condition.

If the fingernails have a sunken, dished profile, look dry and flaking, with vertical ridging, they are reflecting an unhealthy condition. Look to the nutrition for the most obvious answer. It could be that the eating habits are bad, or that a health condition is restricting the body's ability to properly utilise the food it is given. Virgo, Cancer and Ceres aspects would be the first line of investigation, and should suggest if food is the main problem. How does the digestive system deal with analysing the food? How is the person nurtured? Is Saturn, or Neptune, holding back on the self-esteem, making someone feel unworthy of nurture? Has the whole life become so out of control (Neptune) that food intake is the only activity which can be controlled (Saturn)? There may well be an underlying health condition which debilitates the whole body system, and which should lead a person to consult with his medical practitioner.

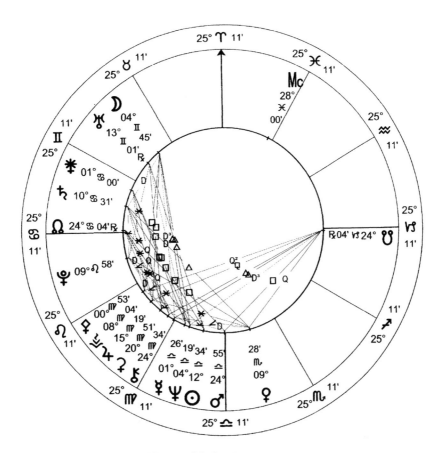

Figure 28 Coeliac chart

Coeliac Disease

Coeliac disease is a condition of the abdomen in which the sensitivity to gluten, and consequent intolerance of it, prevents the proper absorption of nutrients. Figure 28 is the natal chart of a person with this condition. No handprints are available. This is a case where, if the warning signs on the hand had been recognised by medical practitioners, then diagnosis could have been made much more swiftly. Food sensitivity lines, running in from the percussion (Lunar) edge of the palm, could give the first suggestion of a tendency; then the breaking down of the skin ridge

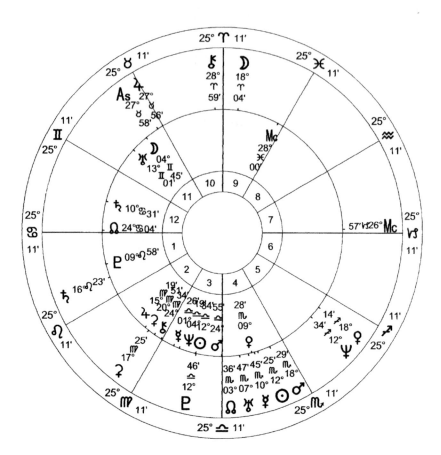

Figure 29 Transits to natal chart

pattern at the top of the Lunar mount, and the presence of a network of very fine lines would point to dietary distress. Since her coeliac condition was diagnosed 30 years ago, and her diet has excluded gluten, the skin ridge pattern is healthy and without the network of fine stress lines. However, the allergy, or food sensitivity lines remain because this is a permanent condition, a lifelong sensitivity.

Nowadays there is a widespread bodily reaction to substances, chemicals and particulate matter, causing breathing problems, skin problems and behavioural problems, even problems with the organs of the body. Food and substance sensitivities are now well recognised by the medical profession. The hand gives a very useful pointer to where the trouble might originate,

Ceres is at 20 degrees of Virgo, in a stellium with Jupiter and Chiron, and within one degree of the Jupiter/Chiron midpoint. They are all in the 2nd house, and in Virgo. By declination Ceres is contra-parallel to Mars; an aspect which is regarded as functioning in much the same way as an opposition. The stressed position of Ceres, goddess of the harvest, whose name is suggestive of a corn crop, indicates where the problem will manifest. Transits to this natal chart, at age 32 are shown in Figure 29.

Virgo is the sign of health, the intestines, and the analysing of foodstuffs by the digestive system. The 2nd house is naturally the province of Venus, with its connection to food and Venus is squared by Pluto, suggesting that there would be a challenge to transform that which is represented by Venus.

Jupiter and Chiron are often in evidence in a healing situation. The midpoint position is a position of stress, and Ceres is within a degree of this position, in addition to being part of the Jupiter-Chiron-Ceres stellium, the conjoining of these energies.

From the time of the first Saturn Return, two years previously, her health had been deteriorating, and when Saturn transited natal Pluto and squared Venus there was a complete breakdown of her system. She was actually starving.

Ceres was transiting to conjunct the Jupiter-Ceres-Chiron stellium, adding focus on itself. Uranus transiting natal Venus brought a sudden shock in the food element of her life. This transit coincided with diagnosis of her illness, enlightenment about her condition. As is so often the nature of a Uranus transit, the answer came from an unexpected source. After senior doctors had failed to find the root of her illness, it was actually diagnosed by a junior doctor.

Pluto transited her natal Sun. The breakdown of her health, which brought a near-death situation, was diagnosed, and her life and body were transformed and rebuilt.

Depression

A depressive condition can be short-term, or long-term. Sometimes a person may complain of depression, when in fact they are just 'fed up', frustrated that they are not getting enough excitement or fulfilment in their life, and generally feeling sorry for themselves. Depression and sadness are not necessarily the same thing. Feelings of misery, disappointment or unhappiness often tend to be transient; the miserable phase passes along with the transits which activated it. The feelings of depression may in fact be as a resistance to dealing with the real purpose of the transit. On the other hand, a long-term depressive condition is a very serious matter, and calls for qualified and understanding help.

Perhaps the natal chart shows a character who lacks the motivational energy to put in all the hard work and concentrated effort needed to bring the desired successful result. Looking at the strength or weakness of Saturn in aspect to personal planets, Mars in particular, may point to whether or not the person is likely to make a sustained effort. If expectation exceeds reality then an over-optimistic Jupiter should suggest it. In aspect with Neptune, the intention may be good, but unrealistic. It could also bring an overconfidence that a gamble will succeed, with a disappointed anti-climax.

Charts which are not well-grounded, particularly if the emotional Water signs are dominant, can incline someone to be overwhelmed by their emotions. This imbalance can bring feelings of depression, which may be also associated with manic periods.

An innate tendency to depression will be suggested in the natal chart. The most obvious combinations of planets would involve hard aspects of Neptune to Saturn, Saturn-Sun, Saturn-Moon, or midpoint configurations of these planets. A debilitated Sun, weak and badly aspected, can lead to a low self-worth and lack of vitality, bringing a person down.

Figure 30 on page 78 shows a low-set 4th (Mercury) finger. The finger may appear to be short, but the length of the finger itself is not the issue. It is set on the palm lower than the adjoining finger, as if reluctant to stand up and make an extrovert communication with the world. Even when the finger stands away from the 3rd finger, indicating independent thought, the setting low on the palm is a clear indication of a fundamental lack of self esteem, and may be the consequence of, say, Saturn squaring Venus or Sun, bringing a challenge to self-worth. As with any hard Saturn aspects, the condition is likely to be chronic, long-lasting, with a tendency to hold on to the past.

Pluto can also show a great difficulty in releasing deeply held and intense pain, and a Moon/Saturn = Pluto (Pluto at the midpoint of the Moon and Saturn) will almost certainly manifest in depressive feelings with enormous difficulty in letting go. A deep, brooding and retentive nature can work itself into a very deep, dark place.

The 'mean hand', figure 25, which illustrates a hand lacking in confidence and courage, shows a lack of joy, and there may be a miserable outlook, which may or may not be regarded as depressive for the person himself. A thumb which clings to the hand and a life line which clings to the thumb show a lack of courage and a repression. Mounts which are not full and fleshy, but which are thin, hard and low show a lack of sensuality. There is a lack of sufficient human warmth to engender a connection with the wider world. This sort of person may actually make others feel drained and depressed.

Transits from the outer planets can be very demanding. They may activate a natal configuration for attention. As one example, the natal chart may have a Saturn square Neptune aspect. If a major transit opposes natal Saturn, then a T-Square is formed, with Neptune as the apex planet, the one most under stress. If the transiting planet were to oppose the natal Neptune position, then. the T-Square is formed, but Saturn becomes the apex planet. Whichever planet is at the apex of this triangular formation is most likely to be the one under most stress, but the whole combination and all it implies will be activated. The difficulty of dealing with whatever matter is brought to attention can be exhausting, and that energy demand can be debilitating and result in a period of depression.

Pluto in particular is known for bringing up deeply buried issues, and forcing the person to deal with them one way or another. The pain of such deep past events or feelings surging up can be quite overwhelming. Resistance can bring a breakdown of health or long-held attitudes, debility and depression at the endings and the death of the old condition, even though the new, transformed, beginnings should be better. The way in which someone handles the trauma affects the outcome and the likelihood of consequent depression. There can be severe and frightening insecurity and fear from the apparent breaking down of some part of the life, leading a person to withdrawal and maybe feel depressed. Whether this time of psychological withdrawal is used for dealing with the problems, or for hiding from them, determines the results.

Transits from Uranus can bring sudden enlightenment, making everything instantly clear. On the other hand there may be such a disruption in a person's life that the shock to the system could be destabilising. Reluctance to respond to a major Uranus transit, desiring stubbornly to maintain the status quo, could show up through Saturn's natal and transiting position, or possibly a strong Taurus-based intractability. Here again, resistance to change can magnify a lack of stability, which may develop as a feeling of insecurity and depression, particularly to someone with a very fixed nature. A major shock can cause the whole nervous system to shut down, and healing can be a prolonged process.

Neptune transits work in a different way. As Neptune dissolves boundaries, so a normally clear-thinking person may become confused and misled. Neptune moves so slowly that its transits last for several years, with no clear moment of beginning or end. The confusion and feelings of loss, and the possible dissolving of the ego, when the Sun is involved, could bring a state of depression with it. Illness and drugs may have to be endured, and the lack of clarity can make a person ungrounded and depressed.

Neptune transits can also be a time of developing intuition, or of unworldly experience of things beyond the conscious boundaries of earthly life. To benefit from these experiences a person must first be well grounded, or the lack of earthly realism can confuse and endanger rational sanity. If drugs become part of the picture, then there may be fearful images, and withdrawal symptoms from the drugs will probably include depression which would be difficult indeed to deal with. The energies of Neptune and Saturn are so very different that combinations of these two planets can be stressful and confusing. They are so difficult to integrate. These planets in aspect in particular are likely to bring with them depression, and even a suicidal tendency, so check carefully the condition of the natal Sun to assess the essential sense of self.

Fine textured skin is common with naturally psychic or intuitively sensitive people, and if accompanied by a hand which is square and practical, then these Neptune transits can be more easily put to good use. If a person is not well grounded then the Neptune transits could carry them into danger.

Depression can also be caused by reaction to certain substances, foods, chemical additives, or drugs, (see Food). Nutritional deficiencies, or hormonal imbalances could also be the source. Thyroid deficiencies cause sluggishness, and can lead a person to feel frustrated and depressed at their own tiredness, and may show as shiny skin on the palms and fingers.

Figure 30 llustrates some marks on the palm which are associated with depression.

a)   The 4th (Mercury) finger is set low on the palm, indicating a lack of self-confidence.

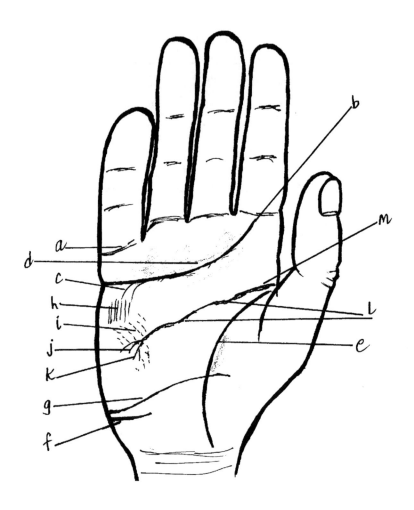

Figure 30 Depression

b)   The Heart line rises high on the Mount of Jupiter, suggesting a perfectionist nature in relationships, doomed to almost inevitable disappointment.

c)   The drooping lines from the Heart Line show deep disappointment in love.

d)   There is a puffiness about the hand, with the Heart line in particular buried deep in the fluid, swollen puffiness. This is a sign that the depression is a long-standing condition, and therefore probably to be seen as a tendency in the natal chart.

e)   The Life line clings close to the thumb, showing a general lack of courage or initiative.

f)   There is an Allergy Line, which suggests that food intolerance may be affecting the mood.

g)   The Via Lascivia, running from within the Life line, on the Mount of Venus, right to the percussion edge of the hand, on the Mount of Moon, suggests that allergic reaction may have led to addiction.

h)   Fine vertical lines rising at the top of the Mount of Moon, under the Heart line, show that stresses are beginning to affect the system.

i)   There is a breaking down of the skin ridge pattern in the Mount of Moon area, suggesting that toxins are undermining the digestive system.

j)   The Head line is frayed at the end, pointing to a lack of clear thinking and concentration, a dissipation of mental energy.

k)   The Head line runs into the Mount of Moon, with no branch rising to balance the imagination. This position is not necessarily any problem, as it shows an intuitive and creative mind, but when it is part of a depressive hand it becomes one more element to be considered, because the imagination may take over. (See Suicide Hand, figure 31.)

l)   Dips in the Head line show periods of depression.

m)   The formation of the Head line is unclear, chained and broken, showing a lack of mental strength or clarity.

Suicidal Depression

Figure 31 shows the hand of a morbidly obsessed suicide.

a)   The whole hand is long and thin and weak, classically referred to as a 'psychic' hand.

b)   The fingers have a ghostly, unworldly appearance.

c)   The Heart line rises high on the Jupiter mount. This suggests someone who puts their idol onto an unrealistic and impossible pedestal, and never recovers from the disappointment when the inevitable happens and the idolised person falls from his pedestal to reveal himself to be only human.

d)   The Life line is weak and frayed at the end, indicating a lack of vitality.

e)   There is a Health Awareness line very much in evidence, and it is frayed at both ends. Expect to see concerns about health matters, maybe even hypochondria.

f)   The Head line begins within the Life line itself, showing a difficulty in standing on her own two feet as an independent person, and a low sense of self.

g)   The Head line sweeps down, right to the lower section of the Mount of Lunar. This is a major sign that the imagination is likely to be morbid and pessimistic. There is no branch of the Head line higher up in the hand, which could introduce a more balanced view of life.

h)   There are fine lines on the percussion edge of the hand, running into the Lunar Mount, suggesting sensitivity to substances or foods.

i)   The Via Lascivia is strongly marked, which tells that her innate ungrounded depressive nature could have been exacerbated by an addiction.

This is the hand of a very ungrounded person.

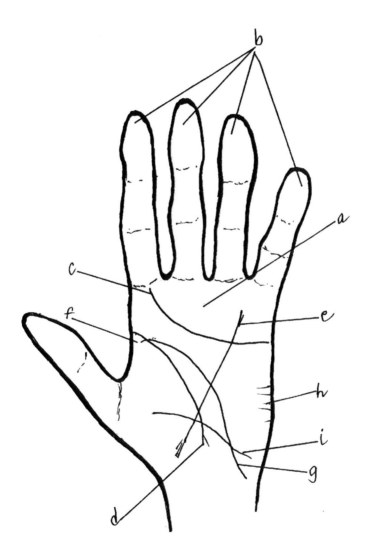

Figure 31 Suicide

PART 2

THE PLANETS

INDIVIDUAL PLANETS

When a planet is strongly placed in a natal chart its particular character will be reflected in the hand. Each planet has its own sphere of influence, which is in turn modified by other planets and angles. The following illustrations show marks in the hand from each planet when it is dominant. The specific areas and lines concerned are the ones which would also display signs of excess or abnormality, in accordance with each chart.

The Sun

As the Sun affects the level of self-esteem and vitality, when it is strongly and well placed the hand will look open, confident and full of vitality, with a strong well-set thumb. The nails should be large and healthy, with visible moons at the base.

a)   The Mounts, especially the Mount of Venus, will be full and firm.

b)   The main lines – Heart line, Head line and Life line, will be clearly marked, free from blemishes or faded areas.

c)   The.Head line will start independent of the Life line, showing a confident attitude. It will skirt round the Mount of Venus without clinging closely to the thumb.

d)   The 4th, Mercury, finger will be set level with the 3rd, Sun finger.

e)   The 3rd finger, the Sun finger, is sometimes referred to as the finger of Apollo. Medical research has confirmed that those who had a high input of testosterone when their bodies were forming tend to have a 3rd finger which is longer than the 1st finger. A longer 3rd finger is also said to represents a good fertility level.

f)   The Sun line is a line which runs vertically up the palm. Its length varies from short and fragmented to one line running the whole length of the palm. It illustrates the capacity to enjoy life and be creative.

g)   Well marked Bracelets are another sign of reproductive health.

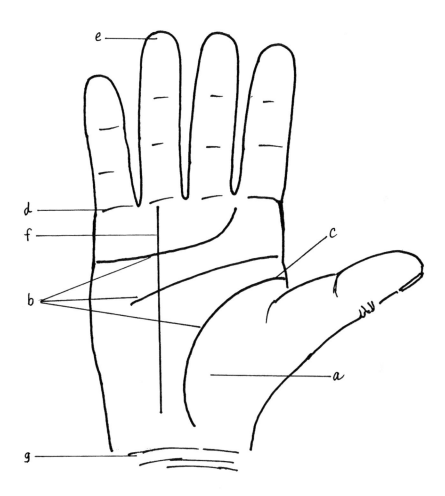

Figure 32 Sun hand

The Moon

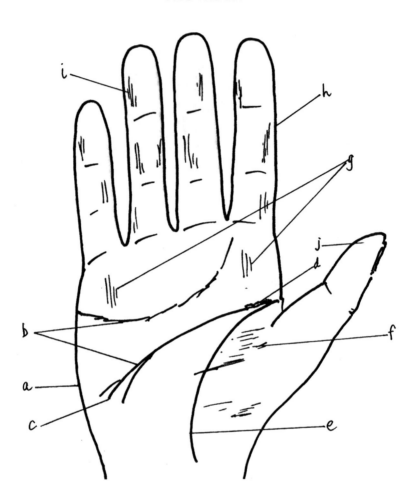

Figure 33 Moon hand

When the Moon has a particularly strong influence in the chart, there will be a much more fluid look to the whole hand. Whereas a strong Sun gave a firm, full character, the Moon's fullness is softer and more watery. It appears weaker and less solid generally, with fewer clear lines and more small, feint influence lines to show the reactive nature of the Moon. It is normal for there to be many small lines on this hand.

a)   The percussion edge of the hand may well show a rounded outline, with a full Mount of Luna.

b)   The Head line and Heart line are curved, with a likelihood of small lines and chaining making up part of the lines. It could be that these small influence lines are attached to an otherwise complete line.

c)   The Head line runs into the Mount of Luna, and may have several branches along its passage.

d)   There may be a chaining at the beginning of the Head line, indicating early ill health, especially when the Moon is rising close to the natal Ascendant.

e)   The Life line will run close to the thumb; a person with a very strong Moon influence is probably more comfortable being influenced by others than expanding themselves out into the world.

f)   The family is probably a very strong influence, and horizontal lines on the Mount of Venus represent influence from the family. If a line here actually cuts through the Life line, then the influence will have escalated into actual interference.

g)   A preponderance of fine lines across the hand probably include empathy lines under the 4th finger and even under the 1st finger.

h)   The fingers do not look very strong, the joints themselves are smooth, showing intuitive thought. Informaton is received directly without ponderous thought.

i)   There are vertical stress lines on the fingers.

j)   The thumb does not jut out assertively, and is rather weak.

Mercury

A strong Mercury influence will show in the hand by marking the areas reflecting mental activity and anxiety. The whole hand may be covered with fine lines, clearer and straighter than those brought about by a strong Moon influence.

a) The fingers are relatively short, with smooth joints; these two factors reflect the speed of thought and communication. Speed of thought does not necessarily reflect intelligence, as indeed much Mercury communication is shallow.

b) The 4th, Mercury, finger is longer in comparison to the others.

c) Below the 4th finger the edge of the hand bulges out with a solid rather than fleshy bump. This is the sign of someone who is a 'fidget', who cannot relax until they have completed all their activities.

d) Mercury is a mental rather than feeling planet, and the Heart and Head lines are clearly marked and straight.

e) The business sense associated with the Gemini merchant is shown by the Head line rising under the 4th finger.

f) The Mounts are thin and firm, rather than fleshy, as this is not a sensual planet.

g) The many different interests of a Mercury-led mind are indicated by a whole series of vertical lines above the Heart line.

h) Both signs ruled by Mercury, Gemini and Virgo, are affected by worry and mental anxiety. The Health Awareness Line, which runs on a straight path up to the Mercury finger, indicates an awareness of health matters. It does not in itself suggest ill health.

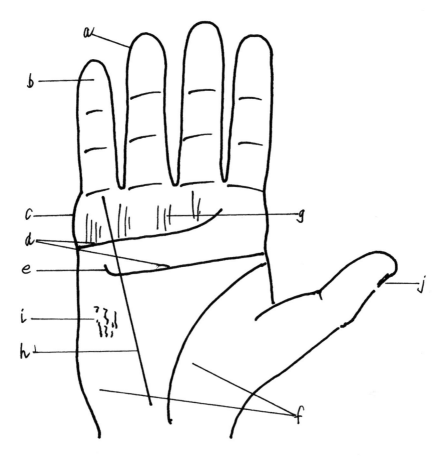

Figure 34 Mercury hand

i)   Anxiety may cause dietary problems, and these are marked by a fine network of wavy lines on the top of the Lunar Mount (see section on Food).

j)   These are the people most likely to bite their nails. Look also for bulbous nails, particularly on the 1st finger, indicating lung problems, another Mercury concern.

Venus

In its purest form, a Venus hand should show a loving nature with a sensual enjoyment of pleasure. The hand itself is attractive, full and warm. There is a suggestion of intractability, a determination to achieve love, harmony and pleasure.

a)   The Mount of Venus is high, firmly fleshy and full, suggesting sensual passion.

b)   The fingers are attractive and smooth, with full basal sections, indicating pleasure in physical matters such as sweet food.

c)   The fingertips are rounded or pointed, and may bend backwards.

d)   The long 3rd finger shows an enjoyment of creativity.

e)   The Heart line is set deep in the palm, an above-average distance from the base of the fingers. This shows a depth of affection. The line itself shows small lines running into it; these are sometimes referred to as 'flirt lines'. They show influences on the affections.

f)   This supplementary Heart line is known as The Girdle of Venus. It reinforces the strength of Venus, as if not all the affection and love could be shown in one line.

g)   The middle joint of the thumb is somewhat pronounced and stiff. Venus rules intractable Taurus and manipulative Libra, determined to achieve harmony.

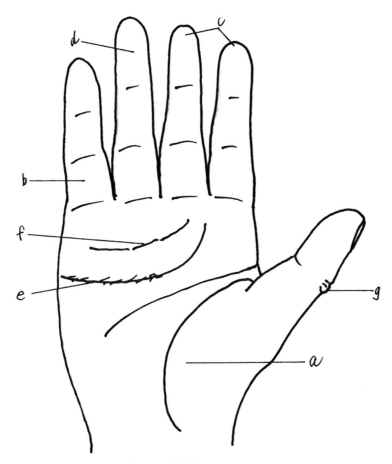

Figure 35 Venus hand

Mars

The Mars hand is strong, firm and hot. The whole appearance is of energy, and strength to use that energy.

a)   The central area of the palm is full and pronounced.

b)   The thumb is set low on the hand and at a wide angle from the palm, showing confident initiative.

c)   Martian wilfulness is illustrated in the strong, firm first phalange of the thumb.

d)   Self-confidence, essential to use Mars energies positively, is shown by a high-set 4th finger.

e)   Capacity for independent action is demonstrated by the 1st finger standing independently away from the other fingers.

f)   The Life line starts high on the hand, confidently separate from the Head line. It runs widely into the palm, leaving space for a full, energetic Mount of Venus.

g)   The presence of the Mars line, on the Mount of Mars Positive, enhances the aggressive qualities of this planet.

h)   An Effort line rising from the Life line and running into the Mount of Jupiter shows   great energy put into an effort to achieve ambition.

i)   When an Effort line running from the Life line stops abruptly at the Head line there is the suggestion that the effort has been or will be unsuccessful, and may cause a loss of status.

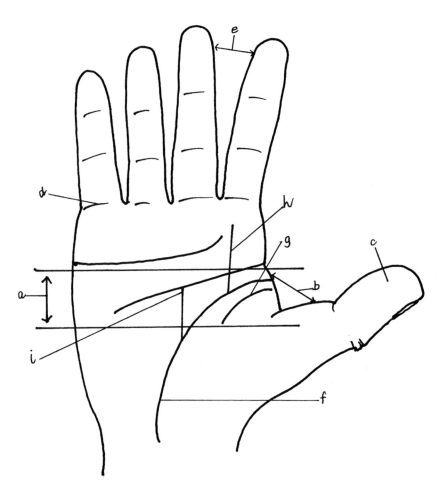

Figure 36 Mars hand

Jupiter

The Jupiter hand has the appearance of being expansive, idealistic and excessive. It can appear rather untidy, with knotty joints to the fingers, and over-developed areas expressing Jupiter's tendency to expansiveness.

a)   The 1st, Jupiter, finger is the largest, with good length and strength.

b)   When the 4th, Mercury, finger is small and low-set, and at the same time the Jupiter finger is more heavily set, there may be a bossy nature which covers up feelings of insecurity.

c)   The finger joints are knotty, indicating a thought process which considers information in an unhurried and philosophical way.

d)   The finger ends are well spaced apart, showing the fiery enthusiasm with which the Jupiter subject reaches out into the world to follow his quest.

e)   Basal finger phalanges are full, indicating excess appetite.

f)   The Jupiter Mount itself is full and firm.

g)   Idealism is shown by the Heart line rising high on the Jupiter Mount.

h)   The Mount of Venus is firm and full, supplying the energy needed to follow the idealistic quest.

i)   The Effort line rising from the Life line onto the Mount of Jupiter reflects willingness and ability to put effort into achieving an idealistic ambition.

j)   The Teacher's Square is common on this type of hand. There is confidence in what has been learnt, and the value of learning encourages the urge to teach others. This is the mark of a good teacher.

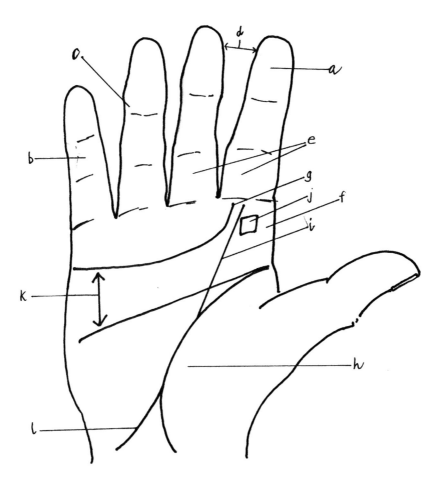

Figure 37 Jupiter hand

k)   The widening distance between the Head line and the Heart line shows an expanding and broad minded view of the world.

l)   The Life line has a branch running into the palm. This reflects the Jupiterian inclination to expand life's experience through contact with foreign people and countries. This branch is often seen on the hands of those who emigrate, or who live abroad for a long period. The original Life line continues on its main path when contact with the mother country is retained, and suggests that the person will return to the land of his birth.

Saturn

The Saturn hand is cool to the touch, with a bone structure very much in evidence. Because it is held in to itself it gives the impression of being narrow and long, without much flesh to the Mounts. Saturn is the planet of old age, and as people age the physical passions tend to diminish and the Mounts tend to lose their fullness, becoming shallow.

a)   The 2nd, Saturn, finger is the longest.

b)   The joints tend to become swollen. They are not knotty in the same way as in a Jupiterian hand, but the joints can become hot with inflamed bones.

c)   The Ring of Saturn, otherwise referred to as The Ring of Solomon, lies at the base of the Saturn finger, said to represent the wisdom acquired during a serious lifetime.

d)   The Heart line is leaning down towards the Head line, indicating that the head, or mentality, rules the heart and has a pull on the course of the emotions. Feelings are controlled by serious thought, and may be pessimistic.

e)   The Head line is straight and unimaginative.

f)   The narrow gap between the end of the Head line and the Heart line represents a narrow vision of life.

g)   The percussion edge of the hand is straight and uncreative.

h)   The Life line clings to the thumb, restraining the space available for the Mount of Venus.

i)   The Mount of Venus is thin and low, and may look somewhat hollow.

k)   Family responsibility is important to the patriarchal Capricornian person, and the strongly etched Family Duty Line expresses this.

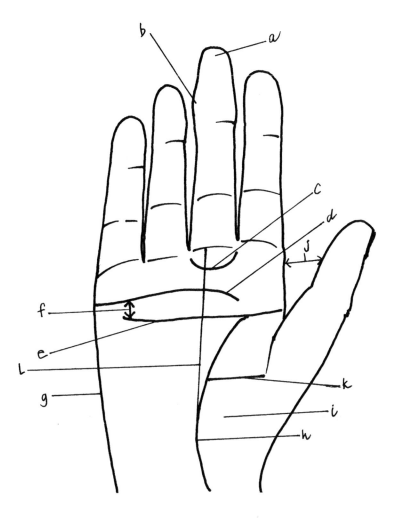

Figure 38 Saturn hand

j)   The thumb is held close to the hand.

l)   The Fate line, running up the centre of the hand towards the Saturn finger, is well marked. Where Saturn is strong this line can start joined to the Life line and continue on a straight, clear path right up to the base of the 2nd finger. This is the case when someone works purposefully for the whole of his life, possibly in what has traditionally been the family business. There is an ingrained 'work ethic'.

Uranus

This hand may appear odd, even eccentric, as if it is freed from the usual restraints of hand formation. The fingers are particularly noticeable in the way they stand apart.

a)   The fingers have smooth sides, indicative of quick, intuitive thought. Uranus is considered to be the higher octave of Mercury with the thinking at a higher, less mundane level.

b)   The 4th, Mercury, finger leans away from the other fingers, indicating independent thought.

c)   The 2nd and 3rd fingers lean away from each other, particularly at the tips. This is the sign of a loner, one who is not emotionally dependent on anyone else.

d)   The 1st finger leans away from the others, indicating independent action. As there is little emotional attachment there is no need to consider others when thinking or acting.

e)   The spaces between the fingers, at their base, is wide. This shows a generosity, a willingness to share knowledge.

f)   The Heart line is clear and uncomplicated.

g)   The Heart line rises on the Mount of Jupiter, an idealistic position, reflecting the idealism felt regarding the belief that all must be for the greater good of humanity.

h)   The Head line is long and clear.

i)   The Head line has a branching line accessing inspiration from the Mount of Luna.

j)   The Mount of Venus is not fleshy and passionate. Uranus is the planet least concerned with earthly pleasures.

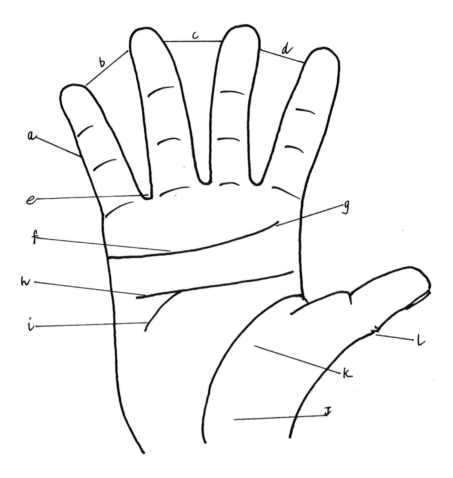

Figure 39 Uranus hand

k)   As Uranus is the planet of the free, inventive spirit, the hand shows no Family Duty lines.

l)   The thumb joint is smooth. As there is no dependency on the opinion or emotions of others, there is no need for obstinacy or resistance to outside opinion.

Neptune

The Neptune hand looks insubstantial, other-worldly and without structure. Soft and flexible to touch, it puts up little resistance to pressure.

a)   Fingers long and thin.

b)   The top phalanges of the fingers are the longest, showing aestheticism and lack of the importance of material concerns.

c)   Neptune is the higher octave of Venus, and as such is concerned with beauty and romanticism. The long 3rd, Apollo, finger reflects this.

d)   The Heart line reflects extreme idealism by rising high on the Jupiter Mount. It does not run a well-marked path, but is subject to unclear sections and a wavering passage across the hand.

e)   Strong feelings of empathy for the fellow man, and a willingness to martyr the self, produce Samaritan lines.

f)   The Head line runs a confused path, with supplementary lines running into the Mount of Luna, accessing intuitive information. The frayed end suggests fragmented thought and lack of concentration.

g)   The Intuition line is a curve which skirts round the Lunar Mount, connecting the Neptune area at the base of the Mount with the Mercury area at the top.

h)   The Lunar Mount is full and curved in its lower section.

i)   This emphasis line runs across the bottom of the Lunar Mount into the Neptune Mount.

j)   The Neptune Mount is not often seen as a fleshy Mount. This area connects the spiritual and psychic intuition of the Lunar Mount with the physical energies of the Venus Mount.

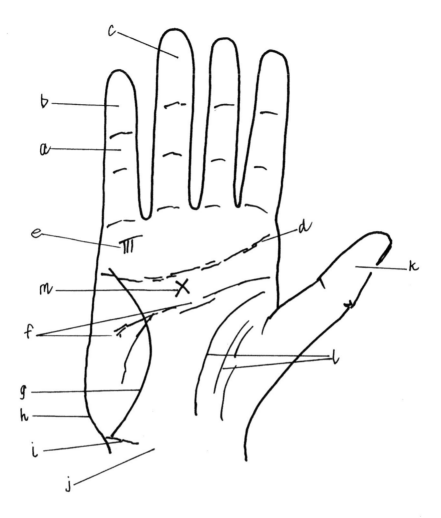

Figure 40 Neptune hand

k)   The thumb shows no signs of aggression, but more the suggestion
     of a personal ego dissolved by Neptune.

l)   The Life line takes a narrow path, and is supported by Companion
     lines, which may represent a belief in the protection by higher
     beings.

m)   The Psychic Cross appears between the Heart line and the Head
     line, and indicates psychic, sometimes mediumistic, ability.

Pluto

A strong Pluto hand is a very powerful one. The firm handshake will hold tight just long enough to test your strength, and to make you aware of its own power. The whole hand appears firm, warm and full.

a)   The thumb has a wilfully determined 1st phalange.

b)   The Mount of Venus is full and very firm, showing passion.

c)   A Mars line runs into the Mount of Mars positive, within the Life line. This Mount is full and firm. Mars is the old ruler of Scorpio, now ruled by Pluto.

d)   The Lunar Mount is fairly full. Pluto can bring intuitive insights, particularly regarding hidden matters concerning other people.

e)   The Heart line is deeply marked, and rises in a sharp curve up to the base of the 3rd finger. Those with this Heart line are more concerned with gratifying their own desires before attending to others' needs. In conjunction with a full, hard Mount of Venus it is indication of an above-average sexual nature.

f)   The Head line runs straight across the hand. This characteristic has been recognised as one sign of Down's syndrome, but it is not exclusive to that condition. It is indicative of the intensity of head and heart working together, and is seen on the hands of many powerful people. Sections of Heart and Head lines may branch from this one straight, intense line.

g)   An ambitious Heart line branches up from the main Head/Heart line.

h)   An intuitive Head line branches down from the main Head/Heart line into the Lunar Mount, giving access to intuitive information.

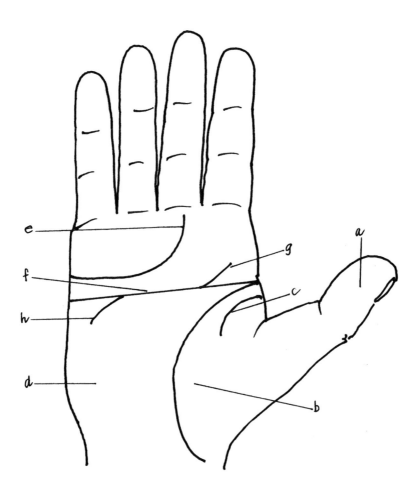

Figure 41 Pluto hand

Chiron

Chiron, 'the wounded healer' has much connection with hands. Incurable wounding, usually early in life, can only be eased by empathising with the pain of others, and can lead people to become healers. Much of this healing is carried out through the hands in the form of spiritual healing and other tactile therapies. Chiropractors, who heal through their hands, chiromancy – the study of the hand, Chiron, the wounded Centaur who became a healer and teacher – all have the same root word. This hand develops warmth and gentle firmness. It can become hot when healing is being practised.

a)   Samaritan lines are the most noticeable feature to be seen on the hand of the healer. They mark the very essence of Chiron.

b)   Fine Empathy lines run vertically on the Mount of Jupiter.

c)   A Teacher's Square often develops here. Chiron was a teacher.

d)   A disturbed beginning to life is shown by chaining at the beginning of the Life line. The Life line and the Head line are conjoined for some length, indicating that the person was not able to make their own way in the world at the beginning, and may be a 'late starter' This running together of the two lines indicates a lack of independence in the early years.

e)   The Life line leaves the Head line and makes its own path, accompanied by Companion lines. These lines show a supporting presence, either a spiritual support or an earthly companion.

f)   Lines running horizontally across the Mount of Venus are evidence of influence from within the family. Here they are cutting through the Life line itself, illustrating actual interference and wounding criticism.

g)   The Heart line shows a fragmented beginning, with a dropping Disappointment line. This is further evidence of early wounding.

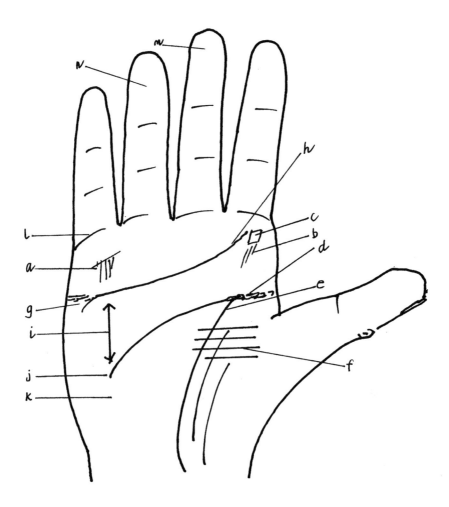

Figure 42 Chiron hand

h)   The Heart line rises idealistically onto the Mount of Jupiter.

i)   The widening space between the Head line and the Heart line show that there is a broadening of the mind, a greater understanding of the world.

j)   The Head line curves sensitively down into the Lunar Mount, to access intuitive knowledge.

k)   The skin is fine.

l)   The 4th finger is low set, reflecting a wounded self-esteem.

m)   The top phalanges of the fingers are the longest, showing that mundane matters are not the most important to this person.

n)   The fingertips often develop raised Droplets, showing their sensitivity to touch, particularly in the case of those who heal through hands-on therapies.

.

PART 3

CHART
AND
HAND
COMPARISONS

CHART–HAND COMPARISON

Example 1

The first glance at figure 43 shows that the planets are evenly distributed with no areas of extremely concentrated energy. The elements are also well balanced.

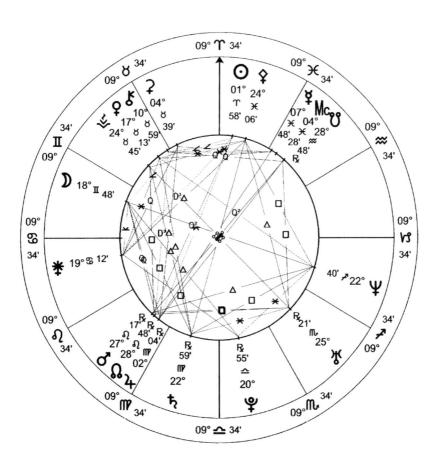

Figure 43 Example 1 'Commando' birth chart

This young man's chart has a Cancer Ascendant, making the Moon the chart ruler. The Moon is in Neptune's natural house, the 12th, and is in opposition to Neptune. Saturn at a 90 degree angle completes this

T-square formation. Neptune's opposition to the Moon gives a suggestion that, for whatever reason, there may have been a lack of clarity regarding the mothering he received. Maybe she was absent, deceptive, or in an intoxicated state, or maybe he had an idealised image of her. With the Moon in the 12th house her inaccessibility might not even be acknowledged, but Saturn at the apex point of this T-square could have brought on some level of emotional depression. Does the handprint show a depressed person, or are there other factors which would overcome this?

Saturn is also the planet at the midpoint position between Mars and Pluto. This would give the young man the determination to overcome any obstacles by working hard. The chart should point to the way in which he overcomes problems, whether in a hard, cold and cruel way as can sometimes be the case with a Mars-Saturn-Pluto combination, or whether this characteristic is softened in any way. The hand should show how Mars/Pluto = Saturn has worked out.

Saturn is trined by Venus, which introduces a stable sense of reality, self-control and dutifulness. The difficulties of Saturn's position are mitigated by the soft Venus aspect. Venus is in quintile aspect to his natal Midheaven, suggesting that, whatever his public standing, he is likely to express his Venus energies in a significant or original manner. The handprint may suggest if his Venus nature is indeed a deep caring one, or not.

This chart has a conjunction of Mars and Jupiter, with the Moon's North Node between them. The Mars-Jupiter conjunction energy is one of the signatures of a good soldier, giving an optimistic and energetic initiative. The North Node position suggests that this could be his karmic path in this life. The square aspect between Mars and Uranus would certainly endow him with the courage and energy to act quickly and decisively in a crisis.

This young man went through a rebellious period when Uranus was transiting in opposition to his Mars-North Node-Jupiter conjunction, and when it hit his Midheaven he enlisted to become a commando. The training of commandos teaches them to use both their head and their heart – that is, both Venus and Mars. The handprint confirms whether he is psychologically qualified for this demanding role.

The Handprint

This handprint of this young man (figure 44) illustrates all the most positive manifestations of Mars energy.

a) The Mars Positive area is very large, with some Mars lines marked. This Mount shows a great deal of physical courage. The texture is firm but it is not in the least hard, which could have suggested aggression.

b) The Mars Negative area, which shows a high degree of moral courage, is also large and clear, with no detrimental markings.

c) The back of the hand has a firm cushion at the thumb joint (not displayed by a handprint, but clear on physical examination). This confirms a good physical robustness.

d) The other Mars area, the centre of the palm, is firm and thick. This again is not illustrated by the handprint, but is clear on physical examination.

e) The thumb stands away from the palm at a very courageous angle.

f) The 1st phalange of the thumb is strong and energetic, and both phalanges are balanced in length. His will does not over-ride his logic.

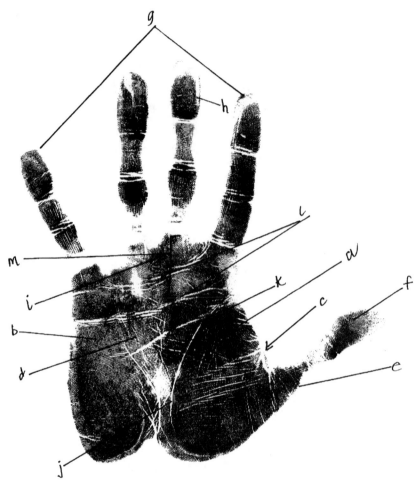

Figure 44 Example 1 Commando left hand

g)   The fingers separate in a confident way, with the 4th finger reaching out in a way that indicates that he can think independently.

h)   The 2nd, Saturn, fingertip has a whorl pattern in the ridges. This reflects the capacity to stick to his own standards of work, and not be swayed. The other fingertip patterns show that his mind is not closed to the opinions of others in his life. In the work (Saturn) area, he can stand firm and determined.

i)   There is a well-formed Loop of Serious Intent.

j)   The Life line reaches out confidently into the palm. At its start it is chained and attached to the Head line, suggesting some early insecurities, but once it comes into its own it is very well marked and clear.

k)   From the point where it separates from the Life line, the Head line is clear and well formed. It has a gentle curve, which would

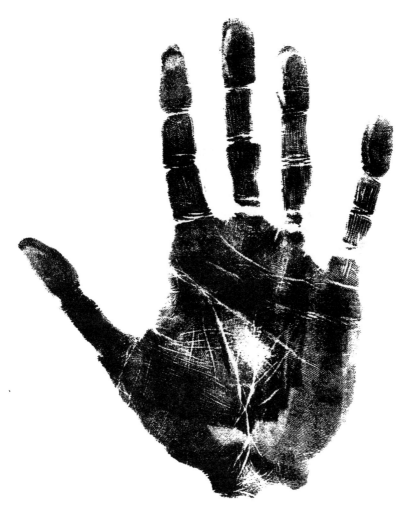

Figure 45 Example 1 Commando right hand

suggest a sensible but feeling thought process. It shows no signs of depression.

l)   He has a double Heart line. This multiplies the Venus caring side of the nature, and softens the Mars energy.

m)   The space between the base of the fingers and the main Heart line is exceptionally deep, showing a greater than average depth of affection and care.

n)   The skin ridge pattern is well-formed and shows no signs of breaking down, another sign of a healthy condition.

In this example, the print of the right hand (see figure 45 overleaf) shows very little deviation from that of the left hand (figure 44), reinforcing the conclusion that this is a strong character who, although sensitive and feeling, has not been swayed by life's experiences.

The strong and healthy Mars energy, along with the depth of concern and the ability to think and act bravely appears to fit this young man for his 'both heart and head' role serving in the commandos.

Example 2

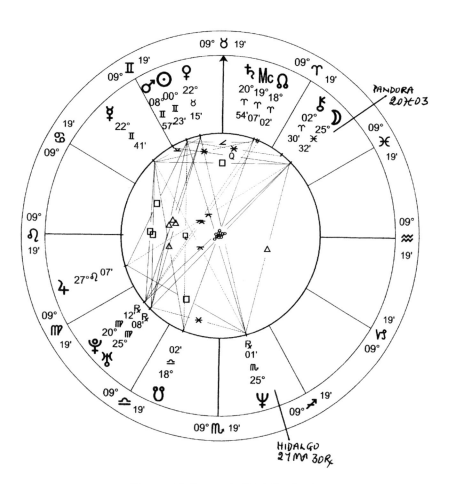

Figure 46 Example 2 birth chart

This lady's natal chart (figure 46) suggests that she has been presented with a rather difficult set of circumstances in this lifetime. There are 2 T-squares, each of which accentuates the other. The first T-square consists of a Pluto-Uranus conjunction opposing a Chiron-Moon conjunction, with Mercury at the apex point. The presence of the Moon in this configuration points immediately to the relationship with her mother. Chiron conjunct the Moon tells us that in some way she has been wounded by her mother; the Uranus opposition suggests that her mother may well have been emotionally unavailable to her, while Pluto in opposition to the Moon suggests that there is some deep dynamic between them which may be unpleasant – she may have been manipulated emotionally on some level by her mother. At the apex point of this T-square is Mercury. It could be that her nervous system was stressed beyond endurance by the parental situation, although Mercury is strong in its own sign of Gemini here. The combined energies of Pluto, Moon and Mercury could have developed as a deeply intuitive thought process.

Looking further into the parental situation leads to the second T-Square. Neptune is in the 4th house, opposing the 10th house Sun, with Jupiter at the apex point in the 1st house. The 4th and 10th house axis represents the parents, and gives more information about whole situation. Neptune, in the 4th house, illustrates the condition of her home life, the mothering she may have received. It is quincunx to Mercury. There is confusion here, possible dishonesty. The male parental principal, represented by the Sun in the 10th house, is opposite Neptune. This suggests that her father was possibly absent, or maybe he was deceived. Jupiter in the 1st house, is the apex planet of this T-square, and adds a suggestion of how she has dealt with the situation She may have been able to use the optimistic influence of Jupiter to rise above and free herself from the situation she was in, or she may have been blindly optimistic that all would somehow be well.

In fact the situation was that her mother lied about the identity of this lady's father. The man who thought he was her father actually was not, and her real father never knew that she was his birth daughter. She was manipulated by her mother to keep this secret.

Her natural intuition is suggested by Mercury at the Moon/Pluto midpoint and is very much enhanced by the fact that Neptune trines her natal Moon, adding a sensitive and empathic nature. Jupiter at the Neptune/Sun midpoint has challenged her to develop an optimistic and positive attitude, looking to a better future. Saturn on the MC will have engendered a wish to appear to the world as a serious person, and its trine to Pluto would have helped give her the ability to work hard and responsibly.

Two asteroids are of significance here. Pandora is close to her natal Moon, and directly in opposition to Pluto, so it becomes part of this T-square configuration. If she had lifted the lid of the box containing her mother's deceit, what mischief would have come out?

The other asteroid worth noting is Hidalgo, conjunct Neptune and opposing her natal Sun. Hidalgo symbolises the defence of one's principles; here at the very base of her chart she found herself unable to stand up for her principles by openly expressing her anger about the family situation. Instead she had to keep quiet, even when, working as a nurse, she attended her birth father in his dying phase.

Chiron in conjunction with her natal Moon will certainly have caused her pain, but it is in Sextile aspect to her natal Sun. The Chiron-Sun Sextile, along with the Neptune-Moon Trine, and the sensitive position of Mercury at the Pluto/Moon midpoint, have led her to use her sensitivity and healing abilities through nursing and holistic therapies. Her principle ambition has been to teach others what she has learned and what she believes in, suggested by Saturn in the 9th house, conjunct her MC. Saturn has brought her to a secure and responsible position in the world, and Jupiter has prompted the optimism and positive outlook necessary to move forward to a better future.

The traumatic situation that she found herself in could have taken a dreadful toll on her emotional stability. The hand prints should show how she has coped.

The Hand Prints

a)   Both the left hand (figure 47) and the right hand (figure 48) show the Life Line chained and attached to the Head Line at the beginning of its course. This is illustrative of the fact that her early

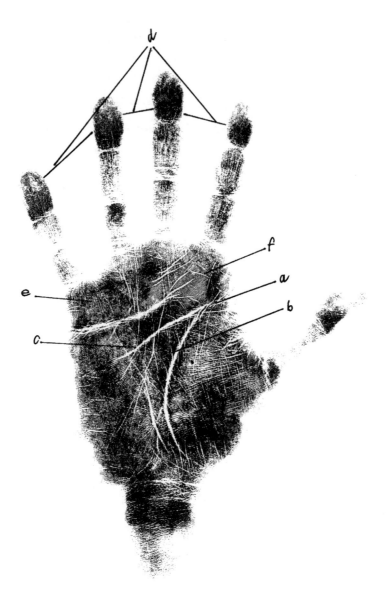

Figure 47 Example 2 Hand print left hand

home life was disturbed, and because of this it was some time before she was able to cope on her own.

b)   The left hand shows a series of effort lines rising from the Life Line, indicating the efforts she would have to make to continue

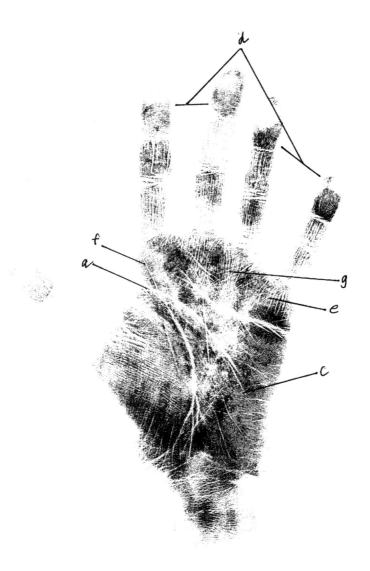

Figure 48 Example 2 Hand print right hand

confidently in life. Some of these little lines start within the Venus Mount, hitting or cutting right through the Life Line, indicating the negative influence from within the family.

c)   There is a noticeable difference between the Head Lines on the left and right hands. On the left hand it shows a slightly undulating passage, with 2 distinct periods of possible depression. It ends high on the Lunar Mount, showing practicality.

On the right hand the Head Line is seen to run a smoothly-curved path into the Lunar Mount. It ends with an extension line running into a loop in the skin ridge pattern. This is a clear indication that she has developed intuition and sensitivity.

d)   On both hands the fingers are seen to be held confidently and optimistically apart, confirming the Jupiterian influence.

e)   Both hands show empathy, or Samaritan lines, but they are not so deeply marked as the lines of the teacher.

f)   On the left hand are marks which show the abilities of the teacher, which could later develop into a complete Teacher's Square. On the right hand the Teacher's Square is seen developing from an ambition line which runs up from the start of the Life Line.

g)   On the left hand are quite a few vertical lines at the top of the palm suggesting a wide variety of interests, whereas on the right hand this feature has developed into a large amount of lines, reflecting the many aspects of therapy and healing which she has studied in order to achieve her ambition of teaching.

Example 3

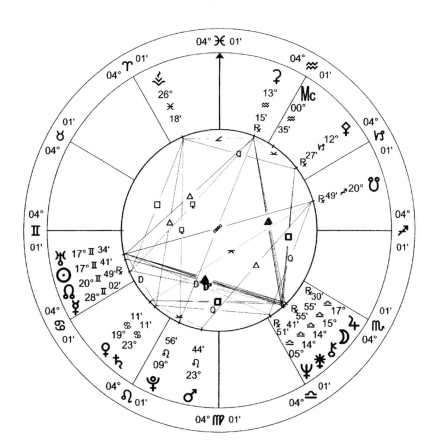

Figure 49 Example 3 birth chart

This natal chart (figure 49) has a disproportionately heavy Air element influence.

All the planetary placements (excluding the asteroid Ceres) are within 120 degrees of arc, suggesting some intensity of experience, with Uranus and Jupiter being brought together by the fact that they are placed at either end of the 'bundle' of planets. This is a good suggestion of a love of freedom and new experience.

The subject is a 'double Gemini', in that he has both the Ascendant and the Sun in Gemini. He also has his ruling planet, Mercury, in Gemini, along with its higher octave, Uranus. This stellium is completed with the Moon's North Node, the point which is said to be a karmic pointer to a life path, and where new experiences are to be had. By declination, Mercury is at a high degree – out of bounds at 25 degrees 10 minutes, adding emphasis to Mercury's function. The whole stellium is in the 1st house of the natal chart and so will represent the person, his physicality and how he faces the world.

The Gemini influence is strong indeed, being on the Ascendant and 1st house, and holding its own ruler, Mercury, and the luminary, the Sun. The conjunction of the Sun with the rising planet, Uranus, is within 7 minutes of arc, and in this prominent position gives the strongest suggestion of an innovative individualist, needing freedom of movement, but having an interest in many things. To what level this is likely to work out will be suggested by the rest of the chart, and by the hand.

The 1st house stellium is in trine aspect to another stellium, this time in another Air sign, Libra, and in the 5th house of creativity and pleasures. At first glance it may appear that here is a very sociable person, loving relationships and friends, but the qualities of the 5th house stellium do actually add a different hue.

The Moon is in this stellium, between Jupiter and Chiron. Jupiter always expands whatever it touches, and so it expands the function of the Moon, the emotional conditioning and habits. How is that Moon aspected? Chiron, the Wounded Healer, is conjunct to within 1 degree of arc. This suggests an inability to function normally on an emotional level, some irreparable emotional damage done at an early age.

Ceres in Aquarius completes a grand trine, adding a suggestion as to what early experience may have damaged the development of a normal emotional make-up. Ceres, as goddess of the harvest, has much to do with nurturing, and Aquarius is a distant, emotionally detached sign. In fact the client's mother placed him in an orphanage and for years his environment was institutional. He was eventually adopted, but was immediately placed in boarding school, and so the impersonal institutionalisation continued.

With so many planets in Gemini and Libra one would expect to see a very person-orientated individual, but there are suggestions that these needs may not be successfully fulfilled. With both luminaries in Air signs there has to be a likelihood of emotional detachment.

The 7th house of partnerships, including marriage, has Sagittarius on its cusp. Its ruler, Jupiter, is part of the Moon's stellium, conjunct the Moon, tied in to and exaggerating the unhappy condition of that Moon.

Venus is conjunct with Saturn in the 2nd house, the house of income and values, including self-valuing. This is not a combination which promises carefree relationship.

There is a major planetary configuration in this chart which probably has had an effect on how he works. Pluto is at the midpoint of Saturn and Mars. This can be a harsh combination. It can give a serious determination to work very hard and achieve what one wants, but it can bring a coldness, even cruelty, to the character.

There is no Earth element in this chart. The only Water element influence is from the Venus-Saturn conjunction in Cancer, which makes the emotional side of the nature very difficult to express. In Fire are Pluto, a generational influence, and Mars. Mars, being part of the Saturn/Mars=Pluto, is probably not going to express a fiery enthusiasm, but more likely an anger which fires the driving determination.

This is apparently the chart of a staunch individualist, certainly with an innovative mind (Uranus). The lack of a stabilising Earth influence would lead to rather a maverick nature.

The Venus-Saturn connection is probably responsible for his craftsmanship, his inventive engineering skill, which is backed up by determined application to the job in hand by the Saturn-Pluto-Mars configuration. The over-loading of the 1st house Gemini explains the tendency to erratic speech, non-stop talking, and the repeating of words to fill any space in time which denies others the opportunity to join in the conversation. In fact, the whole nature is pugnacious.

The planets in Libra, and in Air, may indeed suggest a need for relationship, but the rest of the chart points to why relationships fail.

What does the hand say about the need for relationships? Is this a needy person as far as other people are concerned, desperate to heal the early wound to his emotional system? Is he out and out cruel? Possibly the complete lack of Earth element, and the overwhelming Air element, makes it impossible to come down to a level-headed, well grounded state. This lack of stability suggests that his manic nature could be one way of avoiding depression, the wounded Moon. There is not much stability, and no easy way to be in touch with his own emotions.

The Hand

Example 50 shows that even the view of the back of a hand can give enough information to confirm a natal chart.

a)   There is a pronounced Angle of Proficiency, a sign of a natural craftsman, the Venus-Saturn influence in this case.

b)   The fingers have wide, spatulate tips, typical of a fine craftsman.

c)   There is a creative curve to the Lunar Mount, showing his creative inventiveness.

d)   The 4th, Mercury, finger stands away from the others, showing an independent thought pattern.

e)   The 2nd and 3rd fingers pull away from each other at the tips. This demonstrates that, even though he may think he wants a relationship, his need for independence and space is over-riding, and he does not relate well in a committed two-some. Only with sufficient space could a partnership really succeed.

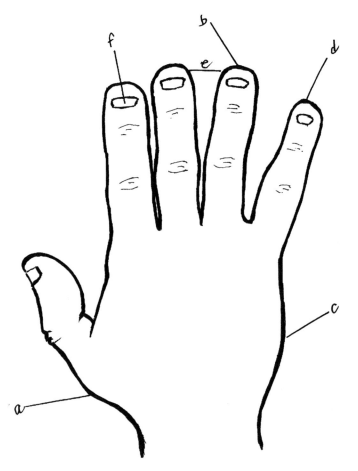

Figure 50 Example 3 Back of hand

f)   The fingernail shape tells much about the emotional state. These
      short, wide nails are typical of a very short-tempered, aggressive
      nature. The nails are also dry and somewhat dished in profile. The
      nervous system is not in a robust, healthy condition.

      The Mounts of the hand are full and hard, and the skin is hard,
suggesting passion but a lack of sensitivity. (This can only be discovered
by physical examination of the hand.)

Example 4

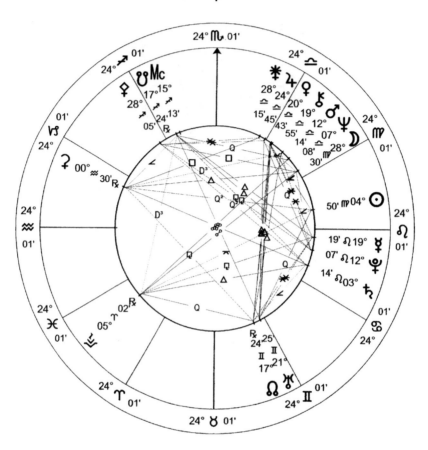

Figure 51 Example 4 birth chart

This natal chart (figure 51) has all the planets in a Bundle of just less than 120 degrees, and all are placed on the eastern hemisphere side of the chart. Ceres is the only body on the other side of the chart and therefore has a special significance in the way it functions; it is like the handle to a bucket, and much is concentrated on that point. This concentration of planets immediately suggests a bias, directing all the energy into one area of life. With all the planets on this side of the chart, this lady is likely to concern herself with other people rather than just with herself. Five planets in Libra compound this need.

The Bundle of planets, with Ceres acting as a handle, along with the strong Libra influence, give parallels to this chart and the previous example, but they function differently.

The 8th house emphasis suggests a tendency to use a relating, sexual, situation to get her own needs met. Libra can be a very charming manipulator, and is after all in polarity with Aries, the 'Me First!' sign. Libra's ruling planet, Venus – the attractive beauty – is placed here in 8th house Libra, and its influence is expanded by its conjunction with Jupiter. Chiron is part of the Libra stellium, and suggests that this lady may be wounded by her Venus activity, or that she may indeed help and heal others by communicating with them, possibly as a counsellor. Reference to the handprint will show if there are the empathetic Samaritan lines on the hand which would give her the motivation to help others in a therapeutic way.

As in the previous chart example, Jupiter and Uranus are brought together not only by their trine aspect to each other, but by the fact that they are at either end of the Bundle formation. This introduces into her character an urge to break away, to have a sense of freedom and a widening of personal horizons. This need for some personal space is compounded by the Aquarian Ascendant, which makes Uranus her chart ruler and thus adds to the Jupiter-Uranus connection. It is at odds with the need for constantly relating with other people which is suggested by the Eastern hemisphere dominance. Venus trines Uranus, which adds to a desire for excitement in love, and the possibility of sudden beginnings and endings because of the need to break away and be free.

Mercury gives a useful indication of the mental condition. It is in Leo, adding Fire and drama to communications. Mercury sits sextile to and at the midpoint of Uranus and Chiron-Venus conjunct. The midpoint position is a point of stress, and this combination could make for nervous agitation. Mercury's position approaching the Descendant adds to her need to communicate with others.

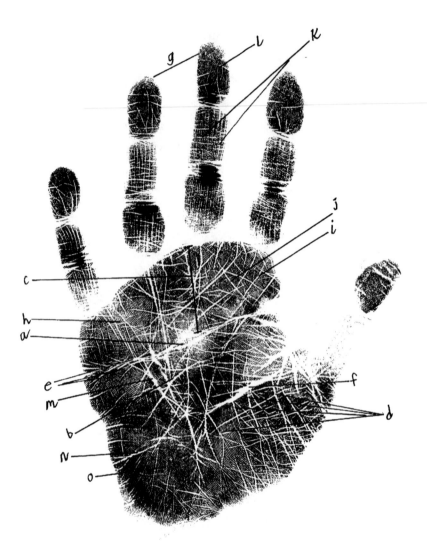

Figure 52 Example 4 Hand print

There is a conflict between needing her own space but also needing to fill her time with other people, and thus constant mental anxiety. In order to find some balance one would look to the Water element signs for some emotional relief, but the Water signs are uninhabited. There are no planets or angles within them, so emotional release is difficult; and this could add to constant mental anxiety. The heavily-tenanted Libra suggests a longing for equilibrium; the hands show whether or not a mental calmness has been achieved.

Both the Sun and Moon are in Virgo. They are the only planetary bodies in the Earth element. The Moon is trined by Ceres, which also opposes Saturn. This combination suggests looking at issues concerning food. It would not be surprising for a Moon and Sun in Virgo person to have food sensitivities, either fussiness, or digestive difficulties. Ceres, goddess of the harvest, adds more importance to the attitude towards food. Virgo is the sign which deals with the digestive system, and its ruling planet Mercury, has already been seen to be in a state of constant agitation. A study of the handprint can confirm the situation here.

The Handprint

Figure 52 shows a large hand, constantly mobile adding drama to speech. Mercury rules the hands, and the restless mobility reflects the condition of natal Mercury, in Leo, on the Descendant, and at the agitated midpoint between Uranus and Venus-Chiron.

a)   The Head line and the Heart line become conjoined, suggesting an intensity to the nature. This is relieved by branches rising as a Heart line and falling as a Head line.

b)   The passage of the Heart and Head lines is not straightforward, and a second, supplementary, Head line starts lower down. It runs into the Lunar Mount, and relieves the intensity of the Head and Heart line combination, but at the same time allowing the imagination to produce more opportunities for anxiety.

c)   The space between the Heart line and the base of the fingers is deep. This points to a caring concern and depth of feeling for others.

d)   The Mount of Venus is full and wide, expressive of 8th house energies. There are many Companion, or Relationship lines.

e)   The Heart line has lines attached to it, giving it the appearance of being chained, but a closer look will show that it runs its length without an actual break, in spite of the disturbances.

f)   There is a strong Family Duty line, to be expected on the hand of someone who needs others.

g)   The fingers are evenly spaced. The 2nd and 3rd fingers do not lean away from each other in a way to suggest a need to be free, nor do they lean towards each other in an over-dependent way. They are well balanced.

h)   There are Samaritan lines to confirm an urge to help others.

i)   A Teacher's Square is marked on the Jupiter mount, showing the ability to help and teach others.

j)   The whole hand is covered by deeply-ingrained anxiety lines. This shows that the hyperactivity and stress is long-term.

k)   There are vertical and horizontal lines on all the fingers, showing a level of stress and tiredness.

l)   The fingertip skin ridge patterns show a good ability to relate to others.

m)   There is a disjointed Health Awareness line, indicating an awareness of health concerns, and possible worry about health, demonstrating the Virgo, Sun, Moon and Mercury placements.

n)   There is a strong Food Sensitivity line.

o)   The skin ridges are in good condition. The Health Awareness and Allergy or Food Sensitivity lines have received attention, and food is controlled (Saturn opposition to Ceres) to the extent that it suits her choice and health.

Example 5

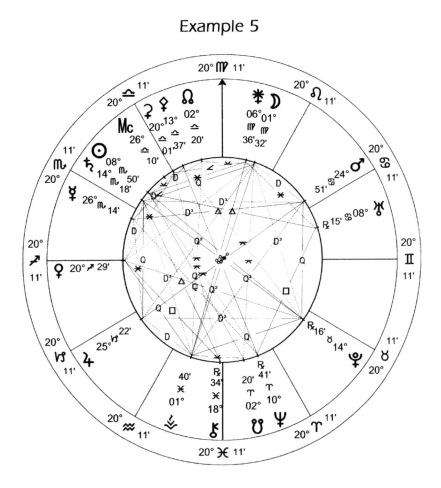

Figure 53 Example 5 birth chart of 'Cheiro'

Figure 53 is the natal chart of Cheiro, a prominent figure in the world of palmistry. He was born in Ireland, in 1866, as William John Warner, of mixed parentage, but became known as Count Louis Hamon, and as 'Cheiro'. The assumed professional name of Cheiro reflects his expertise in the study of the hand, chiromancy. He was a seer, a palmist, astrologer, numerologist, psychic and a clairvoyant. Cheiro befriended and was consulted by many eminent people who were much impressed by his powers, and he read the hands of royals, politicians, military, judiciary and literary personages. He was also known for the exotic decor in his consulting rooms, and for the aura of mystery which he cultivated.

His career included journalism, and he owned two French newspapers which he used to reflect his own opinions. He ran a chemical factory, and was involved in the champagne business. He was also said to have been a Hollywood scriptwriter, and a secret agent for the British Government.

Cheiro was perceived by those who met him as being courteous, charming and enigmatic, but also arrogant and boastful, prone to embellishing his stories. In his autobiographical book "Confessions: Memoirs of a Modern Seer", he claims that he always acted on impulse, and that fate conspired to always present him with just the right opportunity. From reading this autobiography, it does seem that each lucky initiative coincided with a period of financial shortage which prompted him to earn money. Times had been tough at home, and his father was not able to support him, so he left on a ship to India where he began his astrological studies.

In his mid-fifties he retired from giving a reputed six thousand personal consultations each year, and spent his last ten years writing occult books. A look at his natal chart (overleaf) should prove interesting.

The Sagittarian Ascendant confirms his 'foreignness' – he was born in Ireland of mixed parentage, and assumed a non-Irish name, Count Louis Hamon.

A Sagittarian Ascendant makes Jupiter the ruling planet, a very important planet in this chart. It goes a long way to explain his self-inflation. Jupiter in the 2nd house immediately suggests a love of money and spending, his taste for opulence.

Capricorn on the 2nd house cusp, would make for a fear that there might never be enough money, resulting in a strong motivation to accumulate and possess wealth for his own sense of security. His autobiography also revealed that his efforts were usually preceded by a need for money. Jupiter's opposition to Mars would give him the initiative to take immediate advantage of any lucky opportunity. Jupiter is the planet of good fortune, and Mars the planet of will and initiative. The fact that his father did not have the means to support him was what prompted him to take a boat to India and study astrology. This move completely changed his life, and he reinvented himself. Pluto opposite the Sun would explain this personal transformation, his ability to reinvent himself. The hand should confirm it.

Capricorn's ruling planet, Saturn, is conjunct the Sun and opposed by Pluto. The Saturn-Pluto opposition is, of course, a generational influence, and affects everyone born at that time. It is a reflection of the harshness of the period, and can instil a cold determination to transform and improve poor conditions through sustained effort. The Saturn-Pluto opposition in Cheiro's natal chart is within 2 minutes of arc, close indeed, and its connection to the Sun makes it a very strong personal influence. He worked long and hard for his achievements.

The condition of his natal Sun adds some insight into Cheiro's motivation for pushing himself so far from his humble beginnings. Firstly, it is conjunct Saturn. This always gives some lack of self-confidence, and to add in the fact that Saturn's sign, Capricorn, is on the cusp of the 2nd house of values and self-esteem, introduces an anomaly. Was there a need to inflate himself (Jupiter) in order to suppress his innate lack of self-confidence? A look at his hand print may show whether this is a shy man, or an egotist.

The Sun is opposed by Pluto, and is in Pluto's own sign of Scorpio, adding to the Plutonic intense energy. This would lend him a powerful dynamism, to be a man whose presence could have an overpowering and hypnotic effect on others. It would certainly have been one pointer to his success as a hypnotist, as well as his ability to completely change his life and begin again, a reinvented person. It would also explain his work as a government secret agent.

Uranus is the planet of the astrologer. When in aspect to the Sun it can motivate a person to make sudden changes, and to move away

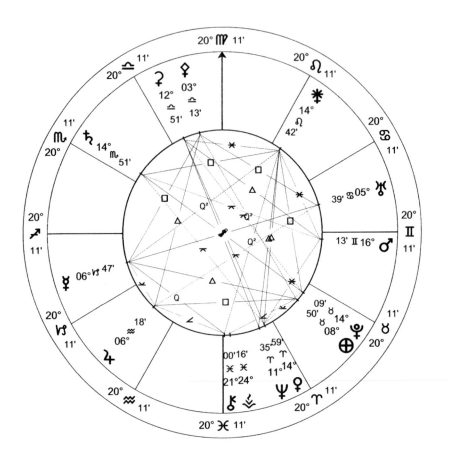

Figure 54 Example 5 Cheiro's heliocentric chart

on their own. Uranus trines Cheiro's natal Sun, and may have given him the urge to leave the parental home suddenly to better his conditions.

Along with his powerful and dynamic personal energy (Sun opposition Pluto), and his capacity for hard work (Saturn opposition Pluto), his bold opportunism (Jupiter opposition Mars), he was helped in his quest (Sagittarius Ascendant), by having Venus as his rising planet. Venus is directly conjunct the Ascendant, rising less than 20 minutes of arc. Libra, the sign ruled by Venus, is on the Midheaven another public position. Natal Venus would help to explain why, even though he was attributed the Jupiterian qualities of boastfulness and arrogance, he was always seen by those who met him as charming and courteous. Venus conjuncts Neptune natally, adding to his fascinating charm and his aura of mystery. As Venus was natally at almost 28 degrees by declination – 5 degrees out of bounds – and as it held such a prominent position in his chart, it is no wonder that he charmed those he met, or that he had such an enjoyment of luxury.

Chiron, rather similar to the word Cheiro, has the same word root from the ancient Greek – *cheir, the hand*. Chiron was not discovered until the 1970s, and so Cheiro himself would not have been aware of the fact that at his own birth Chiron was at the very base of his chart, a deep foundation. It was at that time in the psychic sign of Pisces. His handprint will show if there are Samaritan Lines on the Mercury Mount, indicating his innate motivation to help others, particularly through the hands.

Cheiro's heliocentric chart (figure 54) shows two main focus points. One is the Saturn-Pluto and Earth opposition, touching also healing Chiron and energetic Mars. The other main focus point in this chart is on Neptune, conjunct with Venus. Neptune is at the apex point of a T-square involving a Uranus-Mercury opposition. Uranus is the upper octave of Mercury, so they are closely in harmony. Neptune is the upper octave of Venus, and at this apex point could explain his exceptional psychic abilities. The handprint should show whether his abilities were just a matter of his boasting, or if indeed he was very well developed psychically.

This chart seems to show a man with two characters. One side appears to be a boastful, extravagant social-climbing egotist, and the other side shows a hard-working man, rising from humble beginnings, with a strong motivation to be a healer in his own intuitive way. The handprint may reveal the real Cheiro.

The Handprint

This handprint (figure 55) shows the dual nature of Cheiro, and confirms whether or not this is the hand of a complete egotist.

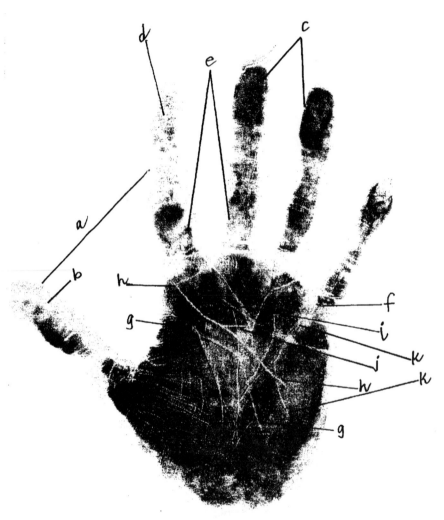

Figure 55 Example 5 Cheiro's hand print

a)   The thumb is at a wide and courageous angle from the palm, but not so widely spaced as to be over-adventurous and rash. (Jupiter-Mars initiative.)

b)   The thumb is strong and long, with a pronounced arrow-headed 1st phalange. This shows the energy he has available to put into his project, and his ability to succeed.

c)   The fingers are well-proportioned, strong, and confidently spaced.

d)   The 1st, Jupiter, finger is pronounced. It stands a little more stoutly than the other fingers, and looks to be wider. It confirms his Jupiterian qualities, including boastfulness. This could be a cover-up for f) below.

e)   The 3rd phalanges of the fingers are long, but not disproportionately heavy. This suggests that opulence and greed for material pleasures was not his major motivation, which could have been as a result of the set of this 4th finger – Saturn conjunct Sun.

f)   The 4th, Mercury, finger is set somewhat lower on the palm than the other fingers, confirming some fear of inadequacy engendered by Saturn's conjunction to his Sun.

g)   His Head line starts its passage closely bound up with the Life line. It was not until early adulthood that he broke away independently on his own. This original Head line dips rather dramatically into the lower Lunar area, not so deeply as to suggest morbidity, but enough to suggest some deep imaginings.

h)   Cheiro is quoted as having said that this second Life line formed after he left home. This is a sure sign of the Pluto-Sun opposition, the reinventing of himself. This Life line rises very high onto the Jupiter Mount. It shows a nature which is ambitious, proud and perfectionist. The line takes a clear path into the intuitive Lunar

Mount. It does not lie straight and over-practical, nor does it rise at the end under the Mercury finger to suggest a high business sense.

i)   The Heart Line is well balanced, not curving up to the 2nd Saturn, finger in a way which would suggest that his own physical desires would have been paramount.

j)   There is a very well-marked Mystic Cross between the Head and Heart lines. This is a sure sign of psychic ability.

k)   Samaritan lines are well marked, his empathy for the human condition and his urge to help others thus confirmed. The Samaritan lines are extended by a line which runs from them and curves into the Mount of Lunar. This is a sign of a highly developed intuition.

CONCLUSION

I do hope that reading this book has helped you to understand just how much information can be gleaned from studying hands. Hands are a most effective means of communication. Even a handshake can tell you whether a person is weak and limp, or whether they want to overpower you.

One very useful technique is to watch the hands of famous people. Newspaper pictures are helpful, but can be misleading at times because of the different camera angles. More information comes from TV coverage, where you can see the hand moving; you can better assess the structure of the hand, and may even get a glance at the main lines on the palm. Compare what you actually see with what you expected to see. Does the hand fit the image? Maybe it reveals what is behind the image.

INDEX

Other books by The Wessex Astrologer

The Essentials of Vedic Astrology
Lunar Nodes - Crisis and Redemption
Personal Panchanga and the Five
Sources of Light
Komilla Sutton

Astrolocality Astrology
From Here to There
Martin Davis

The Consultation Chart
Introduction to Medical Astrology
Wanda Sellar

The Betz Placidus Table of Houses
Martha Betz

Astrology and Meditation
Greg Bogart

Patterns of the Past
Karmic Connections
Good Vibrations
Soulmates and why to avoid them
Judy Hall

The Book of World Horoscopes
Nicholas Campion

The Moment of Astrology
Geoffrey Cornelius

Life After Grief - An Astrological
Guide
to Dealing with Loss
AstroGraphology
Darrelyn Gunzburg

The Houses: Temples of the Sky
Deborah Houlding

Temperament: Astrology's Forgotten
Key
Dorian Geiseler Greenbaum

Astrology, A Place in Chaos
Star and Planet Combinations
Bernadette Brady

Astrology and the Causes of War
Jamie Macphail

Flirting with the Zodiac
Kim Farnell

The Gods of Change
Howard Sasportas

Astrological Roots: The Hellenistic
Legacy
Joseph Crane

The Art of Forecasting using Solar
Returns
Anthony Louis

Horary Astrology Re-Examined
Barbara Dunn

Living Lilith - Four Dimensions of the
Cosmic Feminine
Kelley Hunter

You're not a Person - Just a Birthchart
Declination: The Steps of the Sun
Paul F. Newman

www.wessexastrologer.com